THE FORGOTTEN CHILDREN

A Study of the Stability and Continuity of Foster Care

John T. Pardeck

UNIVERSITY
PRESS OF
AMERICA

Library of Congress Catalog Card Number: 82-20007

This book is dedicated to my father, Kenneth Charles
Pardeck, January 3, 1923 - November 14, 1977.

TABLE OF CONTENTS

LIST OF TABLES

PREFACE

This book is a study concerning the exploration for factors associated with the stability of the foster care experience, a problem that has long been neglected in the professional literature. Stability of care in this research is defined as the number of placements a child experiences while in care.

The neglect of the problem of stability of foster care in the literature makes little sense since it has long been felt that the replacement process has a negative effect on the foster child. Most practitioners feel that such a process disrupts the child's psychosocial development.

The data analyzed in this study was from a larger national study focusing on the kinds of social services children and their natural families receive from the child welfare system. The sample of the present research consisted of over four thousand foster children and their families throughout the United States.

Since the data offered numerous variables concerning each child and his/her natural family, only those variables that appeared to have a logical relationship with the stability of foster care were analyzed. The identification of such variables for analysis was difficult because of the lack of research and theory concerning the stability problem to guide the research process. However, fortunately, the variables chosen in this study for analysis resulted in new insight into the neglected problem of stability of foster care.

It is hoped that a long-term payoff of this research will be to motivate others to further explore the findings. It is also hoped that practitioners and policy-makers will find the results useful for an immediate payoff, that being to help children who are in foster care to lead as normal a life as possible. Since many of these children, the forgotten children, will never be able to leave care because other more desirable alternatives are not available, such as adoption, it appears unwarranted to continue to neglect the problem of stability of foster care -- this study is the first major step toward undoing this neglect. Finally, responsibility for the study's deficiencies is, of course, solely that of the author.

INTRODUCTION

This study follows the traditional process used for approaching a research problem. First, the problem is discussed in detail in Chapter I. What is known about the problem and how it will be approached is covered in Chapter II. The methodology is developed in Chapter III followed by the findings in Chapter IV. The final chapter, Chapter V, discusses the summary and implications of the research.

The implications developed in Chapter V, as well as other results of the study, hopefully will have an impact on those working in the foster care system. One of the implications may be seen as controversial to some practitioners. This implication deals with the finding that most foster children experience stable foster care. As the reader will see, over seventy-five percent of the children in this study experienced stable care. The author feels that this finding suggests that many children in long-term care have no doubt developed important psychological attachments to their foster parents. It is argued that since many of these children will never return to their natural families or leave care, it may be time for the courts to legitimate, through the legal process, the relationship between the child and the foster parents. In essence, by legally recognizing this relationship between the child and the foster parents, the child will finally have a home as most children do. However, as it is well known by practitioners in the child welfare field, foster care is supposed to be a temporary experience. Since it is clearly not, it must be recognized that many children will never leave care and do indeed apparently develop important psychological attachments to their foster parents; the time may have come to redefine the purpose and meaning of foster care. It is clearly emphasized in the research, however, that regardless of whether the system is reformed, the effort to return the child to the natural family must always be the main goal of the foster care system. Only when other outcomes are not possible should the relationship between foster child and foster parents be seen as the best possible outcome for the child.

Finally, the author would like to thank those who supported this work. First, my wife, Jean, provided the long term support needed over the last two years in the creation of this book. I thank Ruth Wachtelborn, my mother, for her encouragement so dearly needed toward the end of the work to make it a reality. Thanks goes to Wanda Witthar for typing the final manuscript. I also thank my colleagues at Tulane University and Saint Louis University for their critical reading of my work and I thank my students who have taken research courses from me over the last two years for their critical analyses of my findings and conclusions. I am deeply indebted to all those above for their help and encouragement.

John T. Pardeck, PhD

August, 1982

CHAPTER I

LOOKING AT THE PROBLEM OF
STABILITY OF FOSTER CARE

Foster care has long been viewed as a temporary service pending a more desirable, permanent arrangement for the child. Research suggests that foster care often times is not a temporary service and for many children involves years of long term care.[1] Unfortunately, this long term care is often an unstable experience for numerous children because of the likelihood that these children will be replaced as time in care increases. The term replacement, within the field of child welfare, refers to the movement of a foster child from his/her current foster home to another foster home.[2]

Ideally, foster care should end with the child returning to the natural family. Normally a child is initially placed in care because his/her natural family is experiencing problems which prevent adequate child care. During this time of placement, the natural family should be receiving family counseling services, typically provided by a child welfare agency. The goal of these services is to strengthen the ability of the natural family to deal with the problems causing the need for foster care. Once the problems for placement are resolved, the child is returned to the natural family.

If it is not possible for the child to return to the natural family, which often times is the case, other alternatives are considered. One major possibility is adoption. Currently adoption is heavily emphasized because of the push for permanency planning in the field of child welfare.[3] The argument for adoption is if a child cannot be returned to the natural family, an adoptive family is far more likely than foster care to provide a conducive home environment.

For many children, a return to the natural family is undesirable or impossible; adoption is out of the question; and other alternatives to foster care cannot be found. Consequently, the child must remain in care. If foster care is the only alternative for the child, a stable foster care experience is seen as a lesser evil than movement of the child through several foster care settings or replacements.[4]

1

Much research has dealt with identifying those factors associated with the foster child who returns to his/her natural family or is adopted.[5] Since these two outcomes of foster care are viewed as positive, it is understandable why they have been emphasized in the research literature. However, little research has been done on the problem of identifying factors associated with stable or unstable foster care. Since for many children foster care is the only alternative, it would seem that more emphasis would be placed on this problem.

The present study is one of the first major efforts to explore factors associated with stability of care, as defined by the number of placements a child experiences while in foster care. The only other relatively major research to explore this phenomenon was conducted by Fanshel and Shinn in their longitudinal investigation of foster care. They state, "The analysis of number of placements experienced by foster children as developed here represents, as far as we know, the first analytic treatment of this phenomenon to appear in the professional literature."[6] Fanshel and Shinn's analysis of the problem of stability of foster care encompassed only a small proportion of the total number of issues reported on in their longitudinal study. Their findings, although limited, will serve as one of the few guides for exploring the problem of stability of care.

Stability of care will be defined as follows: stable care will be viewed as the child who has been placed in one or two foster homes; unstable care will be seen as the child who has been in three or more foster homes. It is quite common for children to experience two placements while in foster care.[7] However, the movement of the child through three or more placements suggests that the child is experiencing unnecessary transfers which disrupt his/her strong need for continuity of environment and continuity of relationships with significant others.[8]

Several studies suggest that an association exists between multiple replacements and the foster child's emotional and behavioral well being. Maas and Engler's research, which reviewed cases of 4,281 foster children, found that children who experienced multiple replacements had a tendency to exhibit more emotional problems than those who did not.[9]

Weinstein reports similar results. In his study of sixty-one foster children, he found a significant relationship between a child's well being, defined as the child's emotional development, and the number of replacements experienced. Weinstein concluded that a high number of placements contributes to poor emotional development.[10]

Fanshel and Maas analyzed the cases of 882 foster children and found a confused self-identity to be associated with a high number of placements.[11]

X Research by Meier of sixty-seven former foster children, consisting of twenty-four adult men and forty-three adult women, discovered, among other things, that an apparent relationship exists between the former foster child's social effectiveness and sense of well being and the total number of placements experienced. Meier found that both men and women experiencing a high number of placements, as compared to those who did not, were less socially effective and generally appeared to have a lower sense of well being. She concluded that a high number of placements has a negative long-term effect on foster children.[12]

The above research on the problems found to be associated with unstable care as reflected through multiple replacements suggests that foster children should be spared unnecessary movement in care.

The Problem

The present study is built on the assumption that the most conducive environment for a foster child is his/her natural family. If the child must remain in foster care and cannot be returned to the natural family or other suitable settings outside of care, such as adoption, every effort should be made to provide the child with a stable foster care experience. This essentially means that the child should experience as few placements as possible.

With the above assumption in mind, the present study will be an exploration of factors associated with stability of care. This exploration of factors will be a secondary analysis of data collected for the National Study of Social Services to Children and Their

3

Families, 1978, by Ann Shyne and Anita Schroeder.[13]
A variety of potential factors will be explored in the
present research which are thought to be associated
with the problem of concern. It is hoped that this
exploration will provide new insight into the problem
of stability of foster care.

Plan of This Study

Since the problem of stability of foster care, defined as the total number of placements a child experiences, has been "under researched," little literature
or theory exists to guide the present study. Also,
the data to be analyzed presents several limitations
as well. As in all secondary analyses, the present
study is confined to those factors available in the
data. Consequently, certain factors potentially related to foster care stability cannot be explored.
However, the extensive nature of the data to be analyzed suggests that a lone researcher limited by time
and money could not possibly gather the amount of data
available in the National Study relevant to the problem of concern.

With the above issues in mind, this research will
be at the exploratory level. The exploration of the
problem of concern will proceed as follows. Chapter
II will present the review of the literature and the
approach to the problem. Chapter III will cover the
methodology and present a series of questions to be
explored based on the approach to the problem developed
in Chapter II. Chapter IV will report the results of
the research findings and Chapter V will present the
summary and conclusions of the study's findings.

Notes and References

1. See, for example, David Fanshel, "Status Changes of Children in Foster Care: Final Results of the Columbia University Longitudinal Study," _Child Welfare_ (March 1976):143-71; Henry S. Maas, "Children in Long-Term Foster Care," _Child Welfare_ (June 1969):213-33; and Alan R. Gruber, _Foster Home Care in Massachusetts_ (Boston: Governor's Commission on Adoption and Foster Care, 1973).

2. Charles R. Horejsi, _Foster Family Care: A Handbook for Social Workers, Allied Professionals, and Concerned Citizens_ (Springfield, Illinois: Charles C. Thomas, Publisher, 1979), p. 134.

3. See, for example, _A Handbook for Social Workers: Permanent Planning for Children in Foster Care_ (Washington, D.C.: U.S. Department of Health and Human Services, 1980), pp. 81-100.

4. Deborah Shapiro, _Agencies and Foster Children_ (New York: Columbia University Press, 1976), p. 70.

5. David Fanshel and Eugene Shinn, _Children in Foster Care: A Longitudinal Investigation_ (New York: Columbia University Press, 1978), pp. 112-37.

6. Ibid., p. 143.

7. Ibid., p. 139.

8. Ibid.

9. Henry S. Maas and Richard E. Engler, _Children in Need of Parents_ (New York: Columbia University Press, 1959), p. 105.

10. E. A. Weinstein, _The Self Image of the Foster Child_ (New York: Russell Sage Foundation, 1960), pp. 66-7.

11. David Fanshel and Henry S. Maas, "Factorial Dimensions of the Characteristics of Children in Placement and Their Families," _Child Development_ 33 (1962): 123-44.

12. Elizabeth G. Meier, "Adults Who Were Foster

Children," <u>Children</u> (January-February 1966): 16-21.

13. Ann W. Shyne and Anita G. Schroeder, <u>National Study of Social Services to Children and Their Families</u> (Washington, D.C.: Children's Bureau, 1978).

CHAPTER II

STABILITY OF FOSTER CARE: WHAT IS KNOWN AND WHAT IS TO BE EXPLORED

The following review of the literature will attempt to draw together what is known about the stability problem as defined by the number of placements children experience in foster care. The review of the literature will be followed by a discussion of the approach to be used in exploring for factors related to stability of care.

Review of the Literature

The literature dealing with the problem of stability of foster care is limited. During the 1950s and 1960s, several case studies are reported in the literature concerning factors associated with stability of foster care as defined by the total number of placements experienced. A limited number of empirical studies can also be found in the literature; however, most of these studies report on single variables, such as age, and their association with the number of placements a child experiences. As mentioned previously, the only study to deal with the problem of stability of care in an analytical fashion is the longitudinal study by Fanshel and Shinn. Shapiro emerges as the only researcher to develop a very limited theory on the problem of concern.

Several studies have reported findings on basic demographic characteristics of foster children and the relationship of these characteristics with replacement. Ambinder, one of the first to study the problem of replacement, analyzed the association of a child's age with the number of placements the child experiences.[1] His study was limited to males between the ages of eight and fifteen years. He divided the children into seven age groups ranging from 8-9 years up to 14-15 years. Ambinder attempted to find whether the age groups differed in number of placements experienced and if a child's age at the time of placement affected the total number of times a child was replaced.

His findings were mixed on the two issues explored. He found that the older age groups experienced more replacement than the younger age groups; however, the initial age at placement has no effect on the total number of placements experienced.[2]

Fanshel and Shinn report extensive findings on the influence of age, sex, and ethnicity on the number of placements a child experiences while in care. Their analysis of these three basic demographic characteristics as related to replacement was accomplished through the use of the multiple regression model.[3]

According to Fanshel and Shinn, the initial age of the child when placed in foster care is not related to number of placements experienced.[4] This finding agrees with Ambinder. They also report that the age of the child is not related to replacement. This finding is inconsistent with Ambinder's research. As reported previously, Ambinder found that as the child grows older he/she experiences more replacement.

The research by Fanshel and Shinn does report that in their initial analysis of ethnicity, they found that black children appeared to experience more replacement than other children. When they controlled for other factors, the relationship between ethnicity and replacement disappeared. They concluded in their findings that length of time in care was the factor causing black children to experience a greater number of placements than other children; that is, black children simply remained in care longer, hence they had a greater chance of being replaced.[5]

However, Jenkins[6] and Sherman et al.[7] report that black children do not necessarily spend more time in care than other foster children. These findings suggest the need for further exploration of the relationship between ethnicity and replacement.

Fanshel and Shinn's findings on sex report that this factor is not related to number of placements experienced. One extremely important finding of the Fanshel and Shinn research related to their analysis of demographic variables and other factors as well is that length of time in care was found to be the best single predictor of stability of care as defined by the number of placements a child experiences.[8]

Another study by Fanshel and Maas reports findings on the factors of age and ethnicity, as related to replacement.[9] These findings were reported as part

8

of a larger study dealing with general foster care issues. Through the use of factor analysis, Fanshel and Maas found that age and replacement were highly correlated; however, ethnicity did not appear to be correlated with replacement. They concluded from the finding on age that the older the child becomes, the more placements he/she experiences. This finding supports Ambinder and in turn refutes Fanshel's work conducted with Shinn.

One important finding also reported in the Fanshel and Maas research is that length of time in care and number of placements experienced by a child were found to be positively correlated. This finding again illustrates the impact of this factor on stability of care and would suggest that length of time in care is an important variable to be controlled for when analyzing stability of foster care.

The literature also suggests a variety of problems confronting not only the foster child, but also his/her natural family, appear to be related to the stability of foster care. The presentation of this literature follows.

Three major case studies are reported in the literature concerning stability of foster care by Littner, Glickman, and Charnley. The central point in all three case studies is that the children who experience multiple replacements all appeared to have emotional and behavioral problems.

The first case to be reviewed by Littner presents a child named Dorothy who is described as having deep-rooted internal conflicts.[10] Littner felt that this internal conflict created a need for this child to be replaced. Littner suggested that this need to be replaced was a kind of "repetition compulsion."

Dorothy's "repetition compulsion" resulted in a total of five different foster homes. In each foster home, she would systematically antagonize the foster mothers and woo the foster fathers, resulting in conflict between the foster parents. Littner felt that Dorothy unconsciously was recreating the kind of home environment she experienced in her natural family.

Littner did find that Dorothy was part of a natural family in which both parents quarreled frequently.

9

He also found that she was close to her father, but not her mother. The conflict between her parents was the cause of her initial placement in care.

Littner concluded that Dorothy, through her "repetition compulsion," was able to recreate in each new foster home what she experienced in her natural family. That is, this repetition of the past helped her to deal with present problems. The need to be replaced, ultimately, helped her to insulate herself from people that she might develop close attachments to.

Glickman's case study discusses a girl named Norma, a child with deep-rooted guilt feelings based on her sense of inferiority which gradually turned to self destructiveness.[11] This self destructive behavior was acted out in each new foster home, resulting in five foster homes in a five-year period. Like Dorothy in Littner's case study, Norma had a fear of developing close attachments to foster parents. Glickman felt this fear was due in part to Norma being raised by her father, whom she felt rejected her by having her placed in care. Glickman concluded that Norma, because of her father's perceived rejection, avoided rejection by others through acting out in each new foster home, resulting in replacement.

The final case study to be discussed by Charnley also presents a child confronted with emotional and behavioral problems which appeared to cause her to be replaced.[12] Charnley took a different perspective than Littner and Glickman on why children with emotional and behavioral problems experience a high number of replacements.

Charnley reports that Margy was clearly an acting out adolescent who revolted against all forms of adult authority. This acting out was not against her parents, because she never knew who they were. Through her acting out, Margy caused four different placements to break down. A decision was finally made to institutionalize her; however, it was decided to try one more foster home first. On the last try, Margy was successfully placed. Her foster parents eventually adopted her.

Charnley felt that Margy's last placement was successful because she accepted the reality of being in foster care. Charnley suggests that a child who is deeply disturbed will many times fight against the initial placement because of the anger and pain felt at the fact of being in care. With each additional placement, the child gradually accepts care. Charnley felt that with children such as Margy, it may take three or four placements before the reality of foster care is accepted.

The above case studies by Littner, Glickman, and Charnley all report a slightly different perspective on how emotional and behavioral problems contribute to unstable care; however, they do appear to agree that these kinds of problems contribute to multiple replacements.

Research by Maas and Engler found that multiple replacements were associated with a large number of children in their sample who were emotionally disturbed.[13] Wiltse and Gambrill concluded in their research that "a disturbed child who enters foster care is more likely to experience numerous placements, and his/her symptoms increase accordingly," thus suggesting that a child's emotional problems may intensify after each new replacement.[14]

Baker and Holzworth found in their sample of seventy boys and seventy-two girls in care that 24 percent of these children experienced three or more foster homes before they were finally institutionalized.[15] Half of these children experiencing three or more placements were placed in care because of delinquency or incorrigible behavior, the other half because of family break-up and parental neglect. The Baker and Holzworth research thus suggests that not only behavioral problems of the child are associated with multiple replacements, but also problems in the natural family.

Fanshel and Maas give further support to the association between emotional and behavioral problems and multiple replacements.[16] They report that children diagnosed as having a "confused" self-identity had a tendency to experience a high number of placements.

Gruber reports in his research sample of 1,721 handicapped children--defined as children having a physical/intellectual impairment or behavioral problem--that they appeared to experience unstable foster care.[17] He concluded from these findings that the child's handicap contributed to multiple replacements.

11

The above empirical studies give further support to the impact of emotional and behavioral problems on replacement. The finding by Baker and Holzworth suggesting problems in the child's natural family also appear to be associated with unstable care leads into the only other research concerning family problems and replacement.

This research by Fanshel and Shinn reports that "family problems" are positively correlated with multiple replacements; unfortunately this study does not define what is meant by "family problems."[18] Fanshel and Shinn do report that abuse, neglect, and abandonment, all characteristics of certain kinds of problems in the natural family, are associated with unstable care. These findings appear to give some support to Baker and Holzworth's research.

Another research finding concerning the natural family also reported in the literature by Fanshel and Shinn is that visiting patterns of the child's parents appear to be related to stability of care. They report that visiting by parents seems to increase the number of placements a child experiences.[19] This finding is extremely important in terms of the positive relationship assumed to exist between parental visiting and children leaving care. Such findings suggest that more research needs to be done on the impact of visiting by parents on all aspects of the foster care experience.

The review of the literature resulted in only one research study attempting to explore the relationship between caseworker characteristics and replacement. This research attempt was by Shapiro. She made the assumption, generally supported within the social work profession, that certain factors such as workers having advanced education and experience and limiting the number of times a new caseworker is assigned to a client, have a positive effect on the helping process.[20] Shapiro attempted to test this very basic theory with four possible outcomes of foster care: (1) return of the child to an improved natural family, (2) stable long-term care, (3) return of the child to an unimproved natural family, and (4) unstable long-term care.[21] Shapiro assumed that the above outcomes of foster care were ranked from the most desirable, return of the child to an improved natural family, to the least desirable, unstable long-term care. The stability of care was defined as the number of placements a child experienced.

Shapiro's exploration of the above outcomes produced fruitful results concerning the return of the
child to the natural family. The more significant
findings were if the worker remained on a child's case,
the child had a greater chance of being returned to the
natural family; also, the more experienced the worker,
the more likely the child was to be discharged from
care to the natural family in the first year of placement.[22] However, Shapiro was not able to explore stability of care with characteristics of the worker due
to an insufficient number of children experiencing replacement in her research population. Consequently an
important assumption of social work practice concerning characteristics of the worker related to stability
of care appears to need further exploration.

Summary

The review of the literature suggests that little
research has been done on the problem of stability of
foster care. The literature reports that two studies
found age to be related to replacement in care; however, a third study did not support this conclusion.
The findings were mixed on the association between a
child's ethnicity and replacement in care. Only one
study reported on the role of gender on replacement--
no association was found between these two variables.

Several studies reported an association between
behavioral and emotional problems confronting foster
children and replacement. Research also suggests that
the child who is handicapped, physically or mentally,
may have a tendency to be replaced. In addition, juvenile delinquency was found to be a factor associated
with replacement in foster care. There is some evidence that certain kinds of problems confronting the
child's natural family may impact stability of care.
Even though the research was not conducted, the literature focused on the possibility that a relationship
may exist between caseworker characteristics and the
number of placements a child experiences. Finally,
length of time in foster care came through as an important factor related to replacement, suggesting that it
is an essential variable to be controlled for in analyzing the problem of stability of foster care.

An Approach to the Problem of
Stability of Foster Care

The nature of this study is exploratory. As the review of the literature suggests, little is known about what factors appear to be related to the stability of foster care. Given this situation, this study will focus on those social components that appear to have relevance for understanding the problem of statility of foster care. The three social components which appear to have particular relevance for guiding the search for these factors are the foster child, the foster child's natural family, and the agency providing the foster care service.

Naturally, the child is a focus of concern because he/she is most involved in the replacement process. The child is the person who must feel the pain of being moved from foster home to foster home. The child is the one who is most affected by a stable or unstable foster care experience. The foster child seemingly is the dynamic having the greatest impact on whether replacement occurs or not. What type of child might this be who is likely to experience stable or unstable foster care?

We have a hint from the literature that the child who experiences unstable care is probably confronted with behavioral or emotional problems. It is believed that these behaviors or emotional problems are not only the cause of replacement, but also the result of it. One would think that the exceptional child--that is, the child with physical or intellectual handicaps-- would be more prone to experience unstable care than other foster children. Such a child is difficult to care for because of unique physical or intellectual problems; hence he/she is likely to experience replacements. Gruber's study did indeed find the exceptional child to be a youngster prone to experience multiple replacements. The literature also infers that the child who is labeled as a juvenile delinquent is likely to experience unstable care. Such a finding appears logical since this child probably exhibits behaviors having an impact on movement in care. In this research, all of the above factors will be analyzed as potential variables related to stability of foster care. The systematic analysis of number of placements experienced with the above problems, so far as known, is the first analytic treatment of such variables to appear in the

14

professional literature.

When considering the social component, the child, the obvious factors of age, ethnicity, and gender also appear to have implications for understanding stability of care. Age of the foster child would appear to be clearly linked to replacement. It would seem that older children experience greater numbers of placements because they probably have been in care longer. However, the relationship between stability of care and age may not be so obvious. Possibly, older children may experience a greater number of placements not because they have been in care longer, but rather because of behaviors resulting from a particular stage of development associated with many trying behaviors that might be a cause for replacement. The past research is far from clear on the association between stability of foster care and age. This study will attempt to clarify the relationship between the number of placements a child experiences in care and age of the child.

Ethnicity and gender are both characteristics found to have an impact on many phenomena in society. A goal of this research is to discover if certain ethnic groups are more prone to experience stable or unstable foster care. The research findings are unclear on this possibility. Gender of the child is also a point of focus. The only other major research done on the problem of concern, the Fanshel and Shinn study, believed this factor to be important; so does the present research. Fanshel and Shinn found the number of placements children experienced and their gender to be unrelated. This study will attempt to see if the present data to be analyzed reflects a similar finding.

The next social component bringing focus to this research is the foster child's natural family. As has been well documented in past research, the family has a tremendous impact on a child's behavior, attitudes, and general development.[23] It is also assumed that the foster child's natural family has an impact on the stability of foster care.

This connection may be interpreted through two potential linkages. First, if the foster child has experienced a home life disrupted by parents with behavioral or emotional problems, it may be difficult for this child to cope with a foster home because of the child's inability to interact with caring adults.

15

Secondly, Kadushin has indicated that behaviors of the
foster child's parents can at times disrupt the ability
of foster parents to care for the child in placement.[24]
In other words, the natural parent may be able to break
down the placement through contact with the child or
with the foster parents. The Fanshel and Shinn research
has given some hint that this second possibility may be
accurate with their finding showing that the more the
parents visit the child, the greater the number of
placements the child experiences.

        Returning to the first possibility, behavioral
and emotional problems confronting the foster child's
natural parents may result in the child having less
than adequate coping skills when placed with caring
adults. Research has reported that children who come
from natural families where they have been abused, neglected, or abandoned have a tendency to experience
replacement.[25] These kinds of problems suggest a
breakdown in parental role performance. Obviously, if
a child comes from a natural family where the parent
has failed in his/her parental role, the child will
probably also have difficulties in role performance.
If the child lacks clear role expectations, the probability of coping with a foster care setting appears
lessened, hence the chance of replacement increases.

        There would appear to be a second level of prob-
lems a step removed from abuse, neglect, and abandonment that are more precise descriptions of problems
facing the natural family and may also be related to
replacement in foster care. These would be the problems that spell out the type of behavioral or emotional problems actually confronting the parent. Fanshel
and Shinn, in their study, give limited support to the
possibility that such problems may indeed have an impact on the stability of the foster care experience.
They found that a very general item defined as a cause
of foster care, "family problems," was associated with
children having a tendency to experience replacement.
Unfortunately, they did not spell out what they meant
by "family problems." However, it can be ruled out
that the "family problems" in their study included
abuse, neglect, or abandonment because these problems
were dealt with as separate variables in their research.

        In this research, an effort will be made to un-
cover particular kinds of problems confronting the
child's natural family that may influence the stability

16

of foster care. The stability of care will be explored in relation to the problems of abuse, neglect, and abandonment, all primary problems as causes of placement in foster care suggesting a breakdown in parental role performance. It is assumed that the linkage between stability of care and these problems is that the child will have developed unclear role expectations for functioning in foster care surroundings, thus setting the stage for replacement.

Other family problems such as alcoholism, drug abuse, and mental illness of the parents will be explored in this study as second level problems. These types of problems will be included in the analysis because they suggest that the child may be coming from a home where adequate coping skills and behaviors, among other things, are difficult to develop. Thus when the child is placed in a foster home, the foster parents may have great difficulty dealing with the child. Furthermore, as suggested by Kadushin, the behaviors of a child's parents may indeed cause a placement to break down. It was suggested earlier that this may occur through the parents' contact with the foster child or even with the foster parents. This study will attempt to discover just what these kinds of problems confronting the natural parent might be that would create behaviors capable of breaking down a placement in foster care. At a less complex level, the effects of contact between the child and his/her natural family will be explored through analysis of the number of placements a child experiences and the visiting patterns of the natural parents.

One final characteristic to be included in the analysis under the social component, the natural family, is an exploration of the relationship between stability of care and intactness of the child's natural family. As reported previously, Baker and Holzworth found in their research that children who had a tendency to experience replacement also had a tendency to come from broken families. A plausible explanation for this finding may again be related to the child's inability to live up to role expectations once in care. The following discussion is similar to the tie developed earlier between replacement and other kinds of family problems; albeit, in greater detail because of supporting literature.

LeMasters has argued that one of the greatest
problems associated with the non-intact family is the
role conflict that the single parent must deal with.[26]
He feels that the single parent role is many times
overloaded or in conflict with other various role commitments. The presence of a spouse allows for more
role flexibility.

The typical foster family that most children are
placed in does not have the degree of role conflict
as would be expected in the non-intact family, according to the LeMasters argument. Most foster families
continue to be two-parent, nuclear systems.[27] Although
agencies do select other kinds of families--for example,
single parent--they do so infrequently, with some anx-
iety and reluctance.[28]

It is difficult enough for the foster child to
learn that appropriate behaviors for the role of foster
child are different from appropriate behaviors for the
role of biological child. This situation may well be
complicated even more so for the foster child coming
from a broken family where role commitments are unclear. When the child is placed in the two-parent
foster family, past role performance may no longer be
appropriate, causing replacement to occur. Kadushin
feels that foster children, through previous experience
in other foster homes, gradually do learn appropriate
foster child role behaviors, suggesting that such a
process of replacement does not necessarily have to be
continuous.[29] With the above discussion in mind, this
research will explore the potential relationship between stability of foster care and intactness of the
child's natural family.

The third social component considered in this
study is the social service agency providing the foster
care service. The agency makes important decisions on
what goals will be developed for the foster child, what
services the child and his/her natural family will receive, and when a child is to be moved from one foster
home to the next. It also attempts to match each foster child with a suitable foster home and will make
the decision of when the child will leave foster care
or if the child must stay in foster care. There would
seem to be within the agency a variety of factors having a potential relationship with the stability of
foster care.

The main thrust of the analyses under this social component will be to discover if the agency appears to react differently to the children who experience either stable or unstable foster care. Practice wisdom and limited numbers of research studies have suggested that children who experience multiple replacements may have special needs, especially in the area of behavioral and emotional functioning.[30] One would assume that these kinds of needs associated with unstable care would be reacted to by the assignment of caseworkers with advanced expertise for dealing with these special kinds of problems. This research will attempt to explore for such a possibility by focusing on particular characteristics of the caseworkers assigned to children experiencing stable or unstable care and the relationship of these characteristics with the stability of foster care.

Only one factor, caseworker turnover, will be explored as a factor having an impact on stability of foster care. Most practitioners believe that the more often a client is assigned to a new caseworker, the less chance the client will have of improving his/her social situation.[31] Shapiro, in turn, hypothesized that caseworker turnover would also have a negative impact on the foster child, by increasing the number of times the child is moved in care.[32] This study will attempt to explore this possibility.

Through the analysis of particular characteristics of caseworkers assigned to children experiencing stable or unstable care, as well as caseworker turnover, a clearer picture should emerge concerning the relationship between these important variables within the agency and stability of foster care. Presently, virtually nothing is reported in the research literature regarding the link between the agency and number of placements children experience in foster care.

The above three social components, the child, the child's natural family, and the agency have defined the focus of this study. Through the defining of the study's focus, certain factors associated with each of the three social components have been identified. These factors will be explored through a series of questions to be developed in the next chapter; through the analysis of these questions, new insight should be gained into the problem of stability of foster care.

Notes and References

1. Walter J. Ambinder, "The Extent of Successive Placements Among Boys in Foster Homes," Child Welfare (July 1965):397-8.

2. Ibid.

3. David Fanshel and Eugene Shinn, Children in Foster Care: A Longitudinal Investigation (New York: Columbia University Press, 1978), p. 143.

4. Ibid., p. 142.

5. Ibid., p. 141-2.

6. Shirley Jenkins, "Duration of Foster Care - Some Relevant Antecedent Variables," Child Welfare 8 (1967):450-5.

7. Edmund A. Sherman et al., Children Adrift in Foster Care: A Study of Alternative Approaches (New York: Child Welfare League of America, 1973), pp. 62-6.

8. Fanshel and Shinn, p. 143.

9. David Fanshel and Henry Maas, "Factorial Dimensions of the Characteristics of Children in Placement and Their Families," Child Development 33 (1962): 123-44.

10. Ner Littner et al., Changing Needs and Practices in Child Welfare (New York: Child Welfare League of America, 1960), pp. 2-35.

11. Esther Glickman, Child Placement Through Clinically Oriented Casework (New York: Columbia University Press, 1957), pp. 263-4.

12. Jean Charnley, The Art of Child Placement (London: Oxford Press, 1955), pp. 86-8.

13. Henry S. Maas and Richard E. Engler, Children in Need of Parents (New York: Columbia University Press, 1959), p. 105.

14. K. Wiltse and E. Gambrill, "Decision-Making Process

in Foster Care," (Berkeley: University of California School of Social Welfare, 1973).

15. John W. Baker and Annette Holzworth, "Social Histories of Successful and Unsuccessful Children," Child Development 32 (1961):135-49.

16. Fanshel and Maas, pp. 123-44.

17. Alan R. Gruber, Children in Foster Care (New York: Human Sciences Press, 1978), pp. 86-7.

18. Fanshel and Shinn, p. 141.

19. Ibid., p. 143.

20. Deborah Shapiro, Agencies and Foster Children (New York: Columbia University Press, 1976), p. 69.

21. Ibid., p. 70.

22. Ibid., p. 89.

23. See R. R. Bell, Marriage and Family Interaction (Homewood, Illinois: The Dorsey Press, 1975), pp. 363-515.

24. Alfred Kadushin, Child Welfare Services (New York: Macmillan Publishing Company, 1980), p. 368.

25. Fanshel and Shinn, p. 143.

26. E. E. LeMasters, Parents in Modern America (Homewood, Illinois: The Dorsey Press, 1977), pp. 134-52.

27. Kadushin, p. 336.

28. Ibid.

29. Ibid., p. 358.

30. Ibid., p. 379.

31. Shapiro, p. 69.

32. Ibid.

CHAPTER III

THE DATA: DESCRIBING THE SAMPLE
AND QUESTIONS TO BE EXPLORED

This research is based on a secondary analysis of existing data collected by the Westat Research Corporation for the United States Children Bureau. The original Westat study entitled The National Study of Social Services to Children and Their Families, 1978, by Shyne and Schroeder is basically a descriptive study. The goal of the original research was to (1) collect comprehensive data on the problems of children and families throughout the United States who receive public child welfare services and (2) improve the survey procedure for obtaining future data on children and families receiving social services.[1]

Description of the Westat Data

The Westat data were collected from only public agencies in the United States. The study focused on these agencies because they provide 96 percent of the social services to children and their families in the United States.[2]

A total sample of twelve thousand children served by these public agencies was drawn from the survey population. This sample of children was generated through a two-stage stratified sampling technique. The first stage consisted of organizing the population being surveyed into appropriate groups. In the second stage, the actual sample elements were selected. This sampling technique, especially for highly heterogeneous populations, reduces sampling error, thus increasing the representativeness of the research sample.[3]

The first stage of the sample design consisted of organizing the public agencies by appropriate geographical areas. This included 101 primary sampling units which encompassed approximately 263 counties and independent cities in forty-one states and the District of Columbia. A total of 286 public agencies were located in the sample area. All of the agencies were asked to participate in the study.

The second stage involved the actual selection of children being served by these agencies. Of the twelve thousand children selected from these agencies, a total of 9,597 completed questionnaires were returned on these children.[4] The questionnaire used in the Westat data consisted of seventeen pages of extensive information for the caseworker to complete about the children and their families.

All of the children in the research sample had to fit within the following categories to be included in the Westat study:

1. Children in placement for whom files were kept

2. Other children who were receiving services for whom files were kept

3. Children from family records where the child was the direct recipient of at least one service

4. Children, other than direct recipients, from family records where the family was receiving related services. In this case, children were sampled based on the number of children in the family (usually one out of each five children was sampled).

The children and families intentionally excluded from the sample were those receiving only health, educational, or financial assistance.[5]

The data were collected between May and October of 1977. In order for a child's case to have been included in the survey, it had to be active on April 1, 1977. For example, if a case was opened in February 1977 and closed during March 1977, it was not included in the research population. The length of time the case had been open was not a factor in sampling, as long as it was active on April 1, 1977.[6]

Since there is diversity in local practices and in definitions for various services and service activities, a definition of terms was included to clarify items used on the questionnaire. Also, efforts were made to clarify terms through site visits to agencies, five regional conferences, correspondence, and telephone contacts with the study's participants.[7]

Description of the Research Sample

In the Westat data, the total number of children who have experienced one or more foster homes is 4,288. These children will be treated as the sample population of the present study.

The children's ages in the sample population range from under one year to seventeen years. The children's mean age is nine. Black children versus white children are overrepresented in the sample in relation to the proportions of both groups in the general population. This is a typical picture of most populations receiving child welfare services.[8] There is a relatively equal distribution of males and females. Approximately one-fourth of the children had experienced three or more foster homes.

Defining Stability of Foster Care

The goal of the present study is to explore factors associated with stability of foster care. As mentioned earlier, an important index of stability of care is the total number of placements a foster child experiences.

One or two placements is normal for foster children. In many instances, when children are placed in foster care, the first placement is often made on an emergency basis. This gives the agency an opportunity to provide temporary care for the child who is unable to be cared for at home and to select an appropriate foster home for the child and prepare the foster home for the child's coming. When the child experiences a third placement, or subsequent numbers of placements, typically these are not by design and may suggest a lack of continuity and instability of care.[9] In this study, one or two placements will be defined as stable foster care and three or more placements will be seen as unstable foster care.

An important factor that will be controlled for in this research is the length of time the children have spent in care. Obviously, the longer foster children remain in care, the greater the probability of movement. Previous research has found that the factor of time in care is the best predictor of stability of care.[10] Time in foster care will be used as a control variable in the analyses of the data whenever there is reason to believe that it may help to clarify a given zero order relationship.

Statistical Test and Measurements of Association

The test of significance to be used in this research to facilitate the analysis of the data is the chi square test of significance. The chi square test was considered to be more appropriate than other tests of significance because the majority of the variables are at the ordinal level. Consequently, the more advanced statistical models of analysis which demand at least interval data will not be used.

The Yule's Q will be the measure of association reported on throughout most of the findings in this study. The gamma coefficient of association will be used where appropriate. In those special cases where the Yule's Q or gamma cannot be implemented, the contingency coefficient measure will be reported on.

The Yule's Q is a special case of gamma. It demands that the two variables being "tested" are dichotomous. The coefficient of association calculated for both the Yule's Q and gamma are roughly equivalent. The values for the Yule's Q and gamma range from +1 to -1: the value of the contingency coefficient depends on table size. The following conventions adopted from Davis will be used in this study for describing the values of the Yule's Q and gamma:[11]

TABLE 1

CONVENTIONS FOR DESCRIBING VALUES
FOR YULE'S Q AND GAMMA

Coefficient Value	Appropriate Phrase
.50 or higher	A substantial association
.30 to .49	A moderate association
.10 to .29	A low association
.01 to .09	A negligible association
.00	No association

Data will be considered statistically significant at the .05 level or less. No initial relationship will be explored further through control variables unless it has reached at least the .05 level of significance.

Approach to the Data

An important limitation of doing a secondary analysis of data is identification of variables in the data which appear to be valid indicators of factors to be explored. Often these variables are readily available in the data; at other times, they are not. The alternative is to use the best indicators available for what is to be measured and explored. Even with the above limitation in mind, a secondary analysis of data is an enormously powerful research approach because it is typically carried out on "data archives" not easily collected by a single person effort. Such an approach facilitates exploration of research questions which would be difficult to investigate by other approaches.

The Westat data offers 279 variables related to issues concerning social services to children and their families. Many of these variables are clear indicators of factors to be explored in this research; others are not. However, for the most part, the data offers an array of variables that can be operationalized to represent the factors of concern in the present research.

The focus of this research concerns the three major social components elaborated on earlier--the child, the child's natural family, and the agency. A series of questions to be explored will be developed. The operationalization of the variables to be explored in each of these questions will be discussed in detail. Throughout most of the analysis, the number of placements a child experiences will be treated as a dependent variable.

The Child

In the Westat data, the problems causing foster care are presented. These problems were indicated by the caseworker assigned to the children's cases. Problems are listed for both the foster children and their natural families.

27

The problems indicated for the foster children
as their reason for placement in care will be assumed
to be the general problems confronting the foster children. Within the data, there are a series of problems
indicated as causes of care that are of relevance to
this study. By exploring these problems, a clearer understanding should emerge in regard to what type of
problems confronting foster children are associated
with the stability of foster care. The problems indicated for foster care will be treated as independent
variables, the number of placements a child experiences as a dependent variable.

The first question explored will try to ascertain
if a positive relationship exists between unstable foster care and behavioral or emotional problems of children. In the data, three kinds of problems clearly
indicative of behavioral problems are presented as reasons for placement in foster care: home behavioral
problems, school behavioral problems, and community behavioral problems. A general term,"emotional problems,"
is also a problem that the caseworker could have indicated as a cause of care. The question to be explored
concerning the problems facing the children is as follows:

1. Is unstable foster care positively associated with
    a child's placement in care due to home behavioral
    problems, school behavioral problems, community be-
    havioral problems, or emotional problems ?

As covered in the last chapter under the social
component, the child, an effort will be made to discover if unstable foster care has a relationship with
foster children who have been labeled as juvenile delinquents. In the data, there are two problems listed
as causes of care that will help to explore this possibility: one is juvenile delinquency as a cause of
care, an exact indicator for the factor being explored,
and the second is placement in care due to the child
being a status offender, a less direct indicator of
juvenile delinquency. The question asked concerning
juvenile delinquency is presented below:

2. Is unstable foster care positively associated with
    a child's placement in care because of juvenile
    delinquency or being defined as a status offender ?

Also to be analyzed is the relationship between stability of foster care and the exceptional foster child. Two problems concerning the exceptional child as causes of foster care are indicated in the data; these are physical and intellectual handicaps. The question asked concerning the above factors is:

3. Is unstable foster care positively associated with placement in care because of a child having physical or intellectual handicaps ?

The final three questions to be analyzed pertaining to the social component, the child, concern the relationship between stability of foster care and the demographic variables of the child's age, ethnicity, and sex. All three of these variables describing the children's demographic characteristics are clearly indicated in the data. The following questions are of concern to this research.

4. Is unstable foster care positively related to older foster children ?

5. Is unstable foster care more likely to occur among children of any particular ethnic group ?

6. Is the number of placements a foster child experiences related to the child's gender ?

The questions developed above focus on the association between factors related to the social component, the child, and the stability of foster care. These questions deal with behavioral and emotional problems, juvenile delinquency, physical and intellectual handicaps, and the demographic variables of the child's age, gender, and ethnicity. This study will be guided by these questions in the exploration of the very important social component, the child.

The Child's Natural Family

The problems listed in the data as causes of foster care which deal with the child's natural family will be treated as the general problems facing the family. These problems are considered to be independent variables and the number of placements a child experiences will be viewed as the dependent variable.

29

As established earlier, it is assumed that there are linkages between these problems and a child's tendency to be replaced.

Three reasons as causes of foster care--abuse, neglect, and abandonment--are thought to reflect a breakdown in parental role performance, thus suggesting the child may have unclear role expectations which increase the chance of replacement. The following question will be explored to ascertain if this relationship exists:

1. Is unstable foster care positively associated with placement in foster care because a child has been abused, neglected, or abandoned ?

A second level of problems confronting the natural family which precisely define why the child has been placed in care will also be analyzed. The problems identified in the data as precise reasons for placement that seemingly have a logical tie to replacement deal with parental alcoholism or drug abuse and other mental health problems. It is assumed that the linkage between these problems and the tendency to be replaced may be twofold: (1) children who are placed in care for these problems in their families may lack, among other things, less than adequate coping and behavioral skills and (2) these kinds of problems may reflect behaviors of parents which are capable of breaking down a foster care placement. The problems causing placement to be investigated are alcoholism of the father or mother, drug addiction of the mother,[12] emotional problems of the parents, mental illness of the parents, and conflict between the child and parent. The question to be explored is as follows:

2. Is unstable foster care positively associated with placement in foster care due to alcoholism of the father or mother, drug addiction of the mother, emotional problems of the parents, mental illness of the parents, or conflict between child and parent ?

Two other characteristics to be explored under the social component, the natural family, are the visiting patterns of the natural parents and the intactness of the child's natural family.

Fanshel and Shinn found that the more parents

visit the child in care, the greater the chance of replacement. It was suggested that the contact between
the natural parents and the foster child may disrupt
the placement. As developed previously, there would
seem to be the possibility that parents confronted with
behavioral or emotional problems who visit their child
in care may increase the chance of replacement more so
than other parents. Such a possibility is not the main
concern of this study; the emphasis of this exploration
will be simply to discover if stability of care and
visiting are related to each other as suggested by the
Fanshel and Shinn research. The question to be analyzed is as follows:

3. Is unstable foster care positively associated with
    the number of times parents visit the child in
    care ?

    The Westat data reports visiting patterns of par-
ents from January 1, 1977 through March 31, 1977, a
three month period. Even though this three month period does not give a complete picture of the number of
times a child is visited while in care, meaningful insight into the potential relationship between these two
factors should emerge from this time period. Fanshel,
in a recent study, used a similar time span to measure
the impact of parental visiting on the child's exit
from foster care.[13]

    The final factor to be researched under the social
component, the natural family, is whether stability of
foster care and intactness of the child's natural family are related. As discussed previously, there is
reason to suspect that the child coming from the non-
intact family may be a prime candidate for replacement.
The question exploring this possibility is:

4. Is unstable foster care positively associated with
    the natural family which is not intact ?

    The variable marital status in the Westat data
has several attributes indicative of the non-intact
family--these are parents married and not together,
and those who are legally separated, divorced, never
married and not together, widowed, deceased, or
"other." These attributes will be collapsed into one
category defining the non-intact family. The attribute
"other" is included because it is assumed to be a familial situation not indicative of two parents living

together. The intact natural family will be defined
as the family in which parents are living together who
may or may not be married.

The Agency

As covered in the last chapter, the social service agency will be mainly viewed in terms of how it reacts to foster children experiencing stable or unstable
foster care. However, one factor, caseworker turnover,
a common characteristic of many agencies, will be analyzed in terms of how it affects replacement in foster
care.

In the Westat data, the factors giving the greatest insight into how the agency reacts to or may influence replacement deal with the social caseworker.
These factors are the educational and experience level
of the caseworker and the number of times different
caseworkers have been assigned to a foster child's
case.

The first question concerning the agency deals
with the association of children experiencing stable
or unstable care with the caseworker's education and
experience level. It is assumed that if the social
service agency is reacting to the problems of children
experiencing unstable foster care, who are thought to
have special needs, the caseworkers with advanced education and experience will be assigned to these children. This assumption is built on the tenet held within the social work profession suggesting that workers
having advanced education and skills are more adroit
at dealing with clients confronted with special problems. With the above issues in mind, the following
question will be explored:

1. Are caseworkers with advanced education and experi-
    ence more apt to be assigned to children experien-
    cing unstable care than caseworkers not having ad-
    vanced education and experience ?

The other factor, caseworker turnover, will be
treated as a variable influencing stability of placement in foster care. Shapiro has suggested that worker stability, as reflected through the number of times
a caseworker is assigned to a child's case, would appear to have a negative impact on the continuity of

foster care. In this study, the association between stability of care and caseworker turnover will be explored to see if the data reports such a finding. The question to be researched is as follows:

2. Is unstable foster care positively associated with caseworker turnover ?

An important factor that will be controlled for if the above variables are found to be related is length of time in foster care. Caseworker turnover and the number of placements a child experiences in care appear to both be factors that would naturally increase in occurence the longer the child is in care. The implementation of time in care as a control variable should clarify this possibility.

In summary, the questions to be researched under the three social components bringing focus to this study--the child, the child's natural family, and the agency--will be explored in the next chapter. Given the state of the research regarding the problem of stability of foster care, this study is largely exploratory in nature. Through the answering of the questions developed in this chapter, greater insight should be gained into a problem which is largely unexplored and of great concern to those working in or with the foster care system.

Notes and References

1. Ann W. Shyne and Anita G. Schroeder, <u>National Study of Social Services to Children and Their Families</u> (Washington, D.C.: Children's Bureau, 1978), p. 1.

2. <u>National Study on Selected Issues of Social Services to Children and Their Families</u> (Washington, D.C.: Children's Bureau, May 1979), p. 1-1.

3. Earl R. Babbie, <u>The Practice of Social Research</u> 2nd ed. (Belmont, California: Wadsworth Publishing Company, 1979), p. 179.

4. Shyne and Schroeder, p. A-2.

5. Ibid., p. A-11.

6. Ibid., p. A-4.

7. Ibid., p. 17.

8. Ibid., p. 30.

9. David Fanshel and Eugene Shinn, <u>Children in Foster Care: A Longitudinal Investigation</u> (New York: Columbia University Press, 1978), p. 139.

10. Ibid., p. 143.

11. James A. Davis, <u>Elementary Survey Analysis</u> (Englewood Cliffs, New Jersey: Prentice-Hall, 1971), p. 49.

12. "Drug addiction of the father" was not included because of the limited number of samples for this category.

13. David Fanshel, <u>Computerized Information for Child Welfare: Parental Visiting of Foster Children</u> (New York: Columbia University School of Social Work, 1980).

CHAPTER IV

THE CHILD, THE NATURAL FAMILY, THE AGENCY -- HOW THEY FIT

In this chapter, the questions of concern in the present research will be explored. Through the analyses of these questions, a clearer picture should emerge of the child likely to experience stable or unstable foster care. However, before these analyses begin, a general overview of the personal characteristics of the research sample is presented.

Characteristics of the Sample Population

Table 2 presents a general picture of the children in the research sample. The characteristics presented in Table 2 are the children's ages, ethnicity, marital status of their parents, years in foster care, sex, and number of placements they have experienced. It can be observed that the Ns (number of sample) vary somewhat for age, ethnicity, sex, and years in foster care. This is due to missing data. The only factor having data on all of the sample, 4,288 children, is the total number of placements the children experienced. The marital status of the children's parents has considerable missing data because the children's records either did not indicate the parent's marital status or the marital status of the parents was simply unknown.

The ages of the children range from under 1½ to seventeen years. The distribution of age groups suggests that there is an overabundance of older children in the research sample; 37 percent of the children are thirteen to seventeen years old.

The majority of the children are white, 59 percent. Black children represent 32 percent of the research sample, and the "other" category, 9 percent. Most of the children had been in care under three years, 56 percent, whereas 15 percent had been in care over nine years.

The number of children of each sex is relatively equally distributed. The marital status of the children's parents suggests that most of the children had natural families not intact; only 18 percent of the

TABLE 2

PERSONAL CHARACTERISTICS OF FOSTER CHILDREN

	N	Percentage		N	Percentage
Age			**Sex**		
0 to 1½ years	242	(6)	Male	2277	(53)
1½ to 3 years	259	(6)	Female	2002	(47)
3 to 6 years	526	(12)		4279	
6 to 13 years	1657	(39)			
13 to 17 years	1592	(37)	**Marital Status of Parents**		
	4276		**Married**		
			Together	388	(16)
Ethnicity			Not together	280	(11)
White	2441	(59)	Legally separated	117	(4)
Black	1312	(32)	Divorced	728	(30)
Other*	358	(9)	**Never married**		
	4111		Together	37	(2)
			Not together	584	(24)
*Hispanic, Asian, Native American			Widowed	260	(10)
			Parents deceased	17	(1)
Years in Foster Care			Other	51	(2)
Under 3 years	2324	(56)		2462	
3 to 6 years	763	(18)			
6 to 9 years	470	(11)	**Number of Placements**		
9 to 12 years	321	(8)	1 or 2	3344	(78)
12 to 17 years	291	(7)	3 or more	944	(22)
	4169			4288	

research sample had parents living together who were either married or not married.

The majority of the children, 78 percent, had experienced one or two placements, or stable care. Twenty-two percent experienced three or more placements, defined by this study as unstable foster care. In essence these findings suggest that the vast majority of these children did experience stable care.

A serious criticism of the foster care system is that it burdens a large proportion of the children in care with disruption and discontinuity resulting from frequent changes in placement. Clearly, the sample upon which this study is based does not support such an alarming picture of the foster care system. A close review of other studies also refutes this criticism. Vasaly analyzed studies of foster care in Arizona, California, Iowa, Massachusetts, and Vermont and noted that 63 to 79 percent of those children studied experienced only one foster home throughout their stay in care.[1] Vasaly reported that only 11 to 15 percent of the children moved four or more times. Fanshel and Shinn, in their study over a five year period, found that 72 percent of their research sample experienced either one or two placements.[2] Gruber also found that only 25 percent of the 5,680 children in his study experienced more than two placements while in foster care.[3] Thus the criticism that large numbers of children in foster care experience a lack of continuity of care appears unfounded.

Even with this brighter picture of the foster care system, as reflected in the research sample and found in other studies, many children still do experience unstable care. Much more needs to be known about these children. The following analyses of the data should provide needed information on the child likely to experience either stable or unstable foster care.

Length of Time in Care

Fanshel and Shinn, in their longitudinal study, found that the most important positive correlate with the number of placements a child experiences is length of time spent in foster care. Such a finding seemingly is not surprising because of the obvious relationship between these two variables, that being the longer the time spent in care, the greater the probability of replacement.

In this study, it was earlier suggested that time in care would appear to be an important control variable in analyzing the present data because of the findings by Fanshel and Shinn as well as its obvious association with replacement. The use of time in care as a control variable in this study should help to clarify the relationship of other factors found to be significantly associated with stability of care. Keeping the above point in mind, the first bivariate relationship to be explored will be the association of time in care with number of placements experienced.

In Table 3, it can be observed that three through seventeen years in care is collapsed into one category. In the initial analysis of the data, this time period was partialed into the following categories: 3 through 6 years, 6 through 9 years, 9 through 12 years, and 12 through 17 years. It was observed for each of these four time periods that approximately 30 percent of the children had experienced three or more placements. These findings suggest that time in care appears to be a dichotomous variable, with the dichotomy falling between under three and over three years. Hence the dichotomizing of years in foster care as reported in Table 3 appears warranted.

Through a closer observation of Table 3, one can see that only 18 percent of children who were in care under three years experienced unstable care as reflected by three or more placements. Surprisingly, over 80 percent of the children experienced stable care as defined by the present study. However, after three years in care, the percentage of children experiencing stable versus unstable care reflects a different picture. Thirty-two percent of the children in care over three years experienced three or more placements, whereas 68 percent experienced only one or two placements. It can be observed that the Yule's Q score is at a moderate positive level and the chi square score is significant at the .001 level.

The above findings appear to have important implications for understanding the impact of time in care on replacement. One implication is that extensive periods of time in care do not necessarily mean

38

the time spent in care, the greater the probability of replacement.

In this study, it was earlier suggested that time in care would appear to be an important control variable in analyzing the present data because of the findings by Fanshel and Shinn as well as its obvious association with replacement. The use of time in care as a control variable in this study should help to clarify the relationship of other factors found to be significantly associated with stability of care. Keeping the above point in mind, the first bivariate relationship to be explored will be the association of time in care with number of placements experienced.

In Table 3, it can be observed that three through seventeen years in care is collapsed into one category. In the initial analysis of the data, this time period was partialed into the following categories: 3 through 6 years, 6 through 9 years, 9 through 12 years, and 12 through 17 years. It was observed for each of these four time periods that approximately 30 percent of the children had experienced three or more placements. These findings suggest that time in care appears to be a dichotomous variable, with the dichotomy falling between under three and over three years. Hence the dichotomizing of years in foster care as reported in Table 3 appears warranted.

Through a closer observation of Table 3, one can see that only 18 percent of children who were in care under three years experienced unstable care as reflected by three or more placements. Surprisingly, over 80 percent of the children experienced stable care as defined by the present study. However, after three years in care, the percentage of children experiencing stable versus unstable care reflects a different picture. Thirty-two percent of the children in care over three years experienced three or more placements, whereas 68 percent experienced only one or two placements. It can be observed that the Yule's Q score is at a moderate positive level and the chi square score is significant at the .001 level.

The above findings appear to have important implications for understanding the impact of time in care on replacement. One implication is that extensive periods of time in care do not necessarily mean

In this chapter, the questions of concern in the present research will be explored. Through the analyses of these questions, a clearer picture should emerge of the child likely to experience stable or unstable foster care. However, before these analyses begin, a general overview of the personal characteristics of the research sample is presented.

Characteristics of the Sample Population

Table 2 presents a general picture of the children in the research sample. The characteristics presented in Table 2 are the children's ages, ethnicity, marital status of their parents, years in foster care, sex, and number of placements they have experienced. It can be observed that the Ns (number of sample) vary somewhat for age, ethnicity, sex, and years in foster care. This is due to missing data. The only factor having data on all of the sample, 4,288 children, is the total number of placements the children experienced. The marital status of the children's parents has considerable missing data because the children's records either did not indicate the parent's marital status or the marital status of the parents was simply unknown.

The ages of the children range from under $1\frac{1}{2}$ to seventeen years. The distribution of age groups suggests that there is an overabundance of older children in the research sample; 37 percent of the children are thirteen to seventeen years old.

The majority of the children are white, 59 percent. Black children represent 32 percent of the research sample, and the "other" category, 9 percent. Most of the children had been in care under three years, 56 percent, whereas 15 percent had been in care over nine years.

The number of children of each sex is relatively equally distributed. The marital status of the children's parents suggests that most of the children had natural families not intact; only 18 percent of the

TABLE 2

PERSONAL CHARACTERISTICS OF FOSTER CHILDREN

	N	Percentage		N	Percentage
Age			**Sex**		
0 to 1½ years	242	(6)	Male	2277	(53)
1½ to 3 years	259	(6)	Female	2002	(47)
3 to 6 years	526	(12)		4279	
6 to 13 years	1657	(39)	**Marital Status of Parents**		
13 to 17 years	1592	(37)	Married		
	4276		Together	388	(16)
Ethnicity			Not together	280	(11)
White	2441	(59)	Legally separated	117	(4)
Black	1312	(32)	Divorced	728	(30)
Other*	358	(9)	Never married		
	4111		Together	37	(2)
*Hispanic, Asian, Native American			Not together	584	(24)
			Widowed	260	(10)
Years In Foster Care			Parents deceased	17	(1)
Under 3 years	2324	(56)	Other	51	(2)
3 to 6 years	763	(18)		2462	
6 to 9 years	470	(11)	**Number of Placements**		
9 to 12 years	321	(8)	1 or 2	3344	(78)
12 to 17 years	291	(7)	3 or more	944	(22)
	4169			4288	

research sample had parents living together who were either married or not married.

The majority of the children, 78 percent, had e perienced one or two placements, or stable care. Tw ty-two percent experienced three or more placements, defined by this study as unstable foster care. In essence these findings suggest that the vast majori of these children did experience stable care.

A serious criticism of the foster care system i that it burdens a large proportion of the children i care with disruption and discontinuity resulting fro frequent changes in placement. Clearly, the sample upon which this study is based does not support such an alarming picture of the foster care system. A close review of other studies also refutes this crit icism. Vasaly analyzed studies of foster care in Arizona, California, Iowa, Massachusetts, and Vermor and noted that 63 to 79 percent of those children studied experienced only one foster home throughout their stay in care.[1] Vasaly reported that only 11 15 percent of the children moved four or more times Fanshel and Shinn, in their study over a five year period, found that 72 percent of their research samp experienced either one or two placements.[2] Gruber also found that only 25 percent of the 5,680 childr in his study experienced more than two placements w in foster care.[3] Thus the criticism that large num of children in foster care experience a lack of con uity of care appears unfounded.

Even with this brighter picture of the foster system, as reflected in the research sample and fou in other studies, many children still do experience unstable care. Much more needs to be known about t children. The following analyses of the data shoul provide needed information on the child likely to e perience either stable or unstable foster care.

Length of Time in Care

Fanshel and Shinn, in their longitudinal study found that the most important positive correlate wit the number of placements a child experiences is leng of time spent in foster care. Such a finding seemin ly is not surprising because of the obvious relation ship between these two variables, that being the lor

TABLE 3

NUMBER OF PLACEMENTS EXPERIENCED
BY YEARS IN FOSTER CARE
(PERCENTAGES)

| Number of Placements* | Years in Care | |
	Under 3 years	3 thru 17 years
1 or 2	82	68
3 or more	18	32
	(2324)	(1845)

Yule's Q=.36 X^2=33.58   df=1   P<.001

*Throughout the tables, 1 or 2 placements represents stable care and 3 or more placements represents unstable care.

a greater number of placements experienced. The chance of a child experiencing unstable care who has been in care at least three years is the same as for the child who has been in care for seventeen years.

If we look to the Fanshel and Shinn study, the above finding does not necessarily contradict their research. As mentioned previously, their study covered a five year period, whereas the present data reports findings on children in foster care up to seventeen years. Consequently, there would appear to be the possibility that the dichotomy reported for under three years in care versus over three years in care may not have been discernible, if present at all, in the Fanshel and Shinn data because of the shorter time period their data was based on. Regardless of this possibility, the variable of time in foster care has emerged as an interesting dichotomous variable in the present research that should be useful in understanding the stability of foster care.

The Child

In the approach to the data, a series of questions were developed under the social component, the child. This section will deal with the findings for each of these questions. The first set of questions concern the relationship between stability of care and various problems confronting the foster child:

1. Is unstable foster care positively associated with a child's placement in care due to home behavioral problems, school behavioral problems, community behavioral problems, or emotional problems ?

2. Is unstable foster care positively associated with a child's placement in care because of juvenile delinquency or being defined as a status offender ?

3. Is unstable foster care positively associated with placement in care because of a child having physical or intellectual handicaps ?

Tables 4 through 7 give general support for the position that behavioral and emotional problems appear to be associated with children experiencing unstable foster care. Table 4 reports a low positive association

TABLE 4

NUMBER OF PLACEMENTS EXPERIENCED BY
CHILD'S HOME BEHAVIOR DEFINED AS
A PROBLEM CAUSING CARE
(PERCENTAGES)

Number of Placements	Child's Home Behavior as a Cause of Foster Care	
	NO	YES
1 or 2	77	67
3 or more	23	33
	(3699)	(589)

Yule's Q=.24 X^2=21.48   df=1   P<.001

between number of placements experienced and the child's home behavior as a problem causing foster care. The percentage of children having "no" indicated for home behavioral problems as a cause of foster care who experienced unstable care is 23 percent, while 33 percent having "yes" checked experienced unstable care. The chi square score reported in Table 4 is significant at the .001 level.

Table 5 depicts the relationship between the number of placements experienced and the child's school behavior defined as a problem causing foster care. The chi square score is significant at the .001 level and the Yule's Q score suggests a low positive association. The percentage of children who had "no" checked for school behavioral problems as a cause of foster care who experienced unstable care was 23 percent, while 31 percent who had "yes" checked for school behavioral problems experienced unstable care.

TABLE 5

NUMBER OF PLACEMENTS EXPERIENCED BY
CHILD'S SCHOOL BEHAVIOR DEFINED
AS A PROBLEM CAUSING CARE
(PERCENTAGES)

Number of Placements	Child's School Behavior as a Cause of Foster Care	
	NO	YES
1 or 2	77	69
3 or more	23	31
	(3775)	(513)

Yule's Q=.20 X^2=12.92   df=1   P<.001

Community behavior as a cause of foster care was the only behavioral problem not found to be associated with stability of foster care. Even though Table 6 suggests a low positive association between number of placements experienced and child's community behavior as a problem causing care, the chi square score is not statistically significant. Hence the findings in this table must be taken lightly.

TABLE 6

NUMBER OF PLACEMENTS EXPERIENCED BY CHILD'S
COMMUNITY BEHAVIOR DEFINED AS
A PROBLEM CAUSING CARE
(PERCENTAGES)

Number of Placements	Child's Community Behavior as a Cause of Foster Care	
	NO	YES
1 or 2	76	71
3 or more	24	29
	(4036)	(252)

Yule's Q=.13 X^2=2.91 df=1   NS

Unstable care, as the past research indicates, is more pronounced among children placed because of emotional problems than for those not placed because of this factor. Table 7 illustrates clearly a moderate positive association between the number of placements experienced and the child's emotional problems defined as a problem causing foster care. The chi square score is statistically significant at the .001 level. The percentage of children having "no" checked for emotional problems as a cause of care who experienced three or more placements is 20 percent; 35 percent of those having "yes" checked experienced unstable foster care. Among the problems analyzed thus far as factors causing care, emotional problems has the strongest association with the number of placements children experience.

It seems reasonable to conclude that children who are in care because of these kinds of problems would be likely to be replaced. No doubt, among other rea-

TABLE 7

NUMBER OF PLACEMENTS EXPERIENCED BY CHILD'S
EMOTIONAL PROBLEMS DEFINED AS
A PROBLEM CAUSING CARE
(PERCENTAGES)

Number of Placements	Child's Emotional Problems as a Cause of Foster Care	
	NO	YES
1 or 2	80	65
3 or more	20	35
	(3180)	(1108)
Yule's Q=.37	X^2=79.46 df=1 P<.001	

sons, these children are more difficult for foster parents to deal with and hence are likely to be moved from
foster home to foster home. Also, as suggested by
Wiltse and Gambrill, each new replacement may very well
intensify the child's behavioral or emotional problems,
thus causing the likelihood of more replacements. Consequently, a reciprocal relationship may well exist between the child's replacement and his behavioral and
emotional problems becoming more severe. Such a phenomena would be difficult to support through survey data
such as this study is based upon; however, the impact
of time in care on the associations found between behavioral and emotional problems and number of placements can be examined to eliminate its effect on these
associations.

     Clearly the research on foster care implies that
behavioral problems of children are related to time
spent in foster care and several studies have supported
an association between number of placements experienced
and emotional problems of children. The research generally shows that long-term care and behavioral and

emotional problems are positively related, that is, children who have these kinds of problems seem to be found in greater numbers among those in long-term care. By controlling for the factor of length of time in foster care, the previous zero order relationships between number of placements experienced and behavioral or emotional problems of foster children can be viewed with more confidence.

The findings in Table 8 show that the low positive association found earlier between number of placements experienced and child's home behavior holds or increases over time in care. For the time period zero through three years, the Yule's Q score is at a low positive level; the Yule's Q score for three through seventeen years is in the high positive range. The chi square score for zero through three years is statistically significant at the .001 level; the chi square score for three through seventeen years is also statistically significant at the same level. This finding suggests that time in care was not the factor causing the original zero order relationship and that child's home behavior as a cause of foster care appears to be related to number of placements experienced.

Similar findings are also reported in Table 9. Table 9 clearly illustrates that the zero order relationship between number of placements experienced and the child's school behavior holds over time. The relationship between number of placements experienced and child's school behavior is at a low positive level for zero through three years and remains at this level of association for three through seventeen years. The chi square score for zero through three years is statistically significant at the .05 level and at the .001 level for three through seventeen years. Again time in care has helped to provide greater insight into a zero order relationship.

The findings in Table 10 also appear to rule out time in care as the reason why number of placements experienced and the child's emotional problems were initially found to be positively associated. Table 10 shows that the association between number of placements experienced and child's emotional problems holds over time in care. The chi square score of 9.25 is statistically significant at the .01 level and the Yule's Q score of .30 indicates a moderate positive level of association for zero through three years. The Yule's

TABLE 8

NUMBER OF PLACEMENTS EXPERIENCED BY CHILD'S
HOME BEHAVIOR DEFINED AS A PROBLEM
CAUSING CARE, CONTROLLED BY
LENGTH OF TIME IN CARE
(PERCENTAGES)

Number of Placements	Years in Care			
	0 thru 3 years		3 thru 17 years	
	Child's Home Behavior as a Cause of Foster Care		Child's Home Behavior as a Cause of Foster Care	
	NO	YES	NO	YES
1 or 2	84	76	71	54
3 or more	16	24	29	46
	(1952)	(372)	(1651)	(194)
	Yule's Q=.25		Yule's Q=.35	
	X^2=13.74 df=1 P<.001		X^2=27.86 df=1 P<.001	

45

TABLE 9

NUMBER OF PLACEMENTS EXPERIENCED BY CHILD'S
SCHOOL BEHAVIOR DEFINED AS A PROBLEM
CAUSING CARE, CONTROLLED BY
LENGTH OF TIME IN CARE
(PERCENTAGES)

	Years in Care			
	0 thru 3 years		3 thru 17 years	
Number of Placements	Child's School Behavior as a Cause of Foster Care		Child's School Behavior as a Cause of Foster Care	
	NO	YES	NO	YES
1 or 2	83	78	70	57
3 or more	17	22	30	43
	(2036)	(288)	(1643)	(202)

Yule's Q=.16
X^2=5.72 df=1 P<.05

Yule's Q=.28
X^2=11.33 df=1 P<.001

TABLE 10

NUMBER OF PLACEMENTS EXPERIENCED BY CHILD'S
EMOTIONAL PROBLEMS DEFINED AS A PROBLEM
CAUSING CARE, CONTROLLED BY
LENGTH OF TIME IN CARE
(PERCENTAGES)

	Years in Care			
	0 thru 3 years		3 thru 17 years	
Number of Placements	Child's Emotional Problems as a Cause of Foster Care		Child's Emotional Problems as a Cause of Foster Care	
	NO	YES	NO	YES
1 or 2	85	74	73	56
3 or more	15	26	27	44
	(1716)	(608)	(1388)	(457)

Yule's Q=.30
X^2=9.25 df=1 P<.01

Yule's Q=.36
X^2=36.15 df=1 P<.001

Q score of .36 is also at a moderate positive level for three through seventeen years and the chi square score of 36.15 is statistically significant at the .001 level.

The above analysis involving the use of time in care as a control variable has helped to increase understanding of the relationship between behavioral and emotional problems and replacement. It is concluded from these analyses that children with behavioral or emotional problems are prime candidates for unstable care.

Next the question of whether foster children who are defined as juvenile delinquents or as status offenders have a tendency to be replaced is explored. Looking at the results in Table 11, it can be seen that the

TABLE 11

NUMBER OF PLACEMENTS EXPERIENCED BY CHILD'S
JUVENILE DELINQUENCY DEFINED AS
A PROBLEM CAUSING CARE
(PERCENTAGES)

Number of Placements	Child's Juvenile Delinquency as a Cause of Foster Care	
	NO	YES
1 or 2	76	70
3 or more	24	30
	(4113)	(175)
Yule's Q=.15	X^2=2.35 df=1 NS	

Yule's Q score is in the low positive range. The percentage of children having "no" indicated for juvenile delinquency who experienced unstable care is 24 percent, with 30 percent having "yes" checked experiencing unstable care. However, the chi square score reported in this table is not statistically significant. Therefore, the findings in Table 11 may be due to chance.

The results for status offender as a cause of foster care are similar to those reported for juvenile
delinquency. In Table 12, the Yule's Q score of .15
suggests a low positive association between number of

TABLE 12

NUMBER OF PLACEMENTS EXPERIENCED BY CHILD
BEING A STATUS OFFENDER DEFINED
AS A CAUSE OF CARE
(PERCENTAGES)

Number of Placements	Child Being a Status Offender as a Cause of Foster Care	
	NO	YES
1 or 2	76	70
3 or more	24	30
	(4073)	(215)
Yule's Q=.15	X^2=2.71 df=1 NS	

placements experienced and status offender as a cause
of care. The percentage of children having "no" checked
for this problem who had three or more placements is 24
percent, with 30 percent of those with "yes" checked
having unstable care. However, the chi square score is
not statistically significant, thus implying that the
findings in Table 12 may also be due to chance.

Even though the findings report that children who
experience unstable foster care have a tendency to be
involved with the legal system, the possibility that
such a finding may be due to chance implies that it
should be taken lightly. Consequently, it is concluded
that the data does not support the past research findings concerning this issue.

The final question to be explored regarding problems facing the children defined as causes of foster
care deals with the possibility of whether exceptional
children, children who are physically or intellectually

handicapped, appear to experience greater numbers of placements than other children.

Table 13, which describes the association between number of placements experienced and physical handicap of the child defined as a cause of care, illustrates clearly that an association does not exist between these two factors. The Yule's Q score of -.06 is in the negligible range. Table 13 shows that 24 percent of the children who had "no" indicated for this problem experienced unstable care, whereas 22 percent who had "yes" checked had unstable care; only a difference of 2 percent exists between these two categories. The chi square score of .31 is not significant.

TABLE 13

NUMBER OF PLACEMENTS EXPERIENCED BY
PHYSICAL HANDICAP OF CHILD
DEFINED AS A CAUSE OF CARE
(PERCENTAGES)

Number of Placements	Child's Physical Handicap as a Cause of Foster Care	
	NO	YES
1 or 2	76	78
3 or more	24	22
	(4058)	(230)
Yule's Q=-.06	X^2=.31 df=1 NS	

The findings also do not support an association between stability of care and mental retardation of the child. In Table 14, a negligible Yule's Q score of .05 is reported with a chi square score of .58, which is not statistically significant. The percentage of children having "no" checked for this problem who experienced unstable care is 24 percent, while only 26 percent of those with "yes" checked had unstable care. Consequently, the analyses of the findings in Tables 13 and 14 suggest that the exceptional child, defined as the child confronted with a physical or mental handicap, does not necessarily have a tendency toward unstable foster care.[4]

TABLE 14

NUMBER OF PLACEMENTS EXPERIENCED BY CHILD'S
MENTAL RETARDATION DEFINED AS
A PROBLEM CAUSING CARE
(PERCENTAGES)

Number of Placements	Child's Mental Retardation as a Cause of Foster Care	
	NO	YES
1 or 2	76	74
3 or more	24	26
	(3939)	(349)
Yule's Q=.05	X^2=.58 df=1 NS	

The final three questions to be analyzed in this section focus on three basic demographic characteristics describing the foster children: their ages, ethnicity, and sex. This set of questions concerns the relationship between stability of care and these three demographic variables:[5]

4. Is unstable foster care positively related to older foster children ?

5. Is unstable foster care more likely to occur among children of any particular ethnic group ?

6. Is the number of placements a foster child experiences related to the child's gender ?

Table 15, which describes the relationship between number of placements experienced and age of the foster child, reports a gamma score of .39 and a chi square score of 74.87, which is statistically significant at the .001 level. This finding clearly indicates a

51

TABLE 15

NUMBER OF PLACEMENTS EXPERIENCED
BY AGE OF FOSTER CHILD
(PERCENTAGES)

Number of Placements	Age of Foster Child				
	0-1½ years	1½-3 years	3-6 years	6-13 years	13-17 years
1 or 2	95	87	79	75	71
3 or more	5	13	21	25	29
	(242)	(259)	(526)	(1657)	(1592)

$G=.39$ $X^2=74.87$ $df=4$ $P<.001$

positive moderate association between the number of
placements experienced and age of the foster child. It
can be observed that the percentage of children experiencing unstable care increases gradually from 5 percent
for children zero to 1½ years of age up to 29 percent
for children in the thirteen to seventeen year old
group. These findings support the research by Ambinder,
and Fanshel and Maas.

In Table 16, which depicts the association between
number of placements experienced and age of the foster
child, controlled by length of time in care, the use
of time in care as a control variable appears to add
additional insight into the original bivariate relationship found between number of placements experienced
and age of the foster child. For the time period zero
through three years, the gamma score is reduced to a
negligible level and to a low positive level for three
through seventeen years. The chi square scores are
statistically significant at the .001 level for both
time periods. These findings imply that time spent
in care specifies when age has an impact on the number
of placements foster children experience. The results
in Table 16 give tentative support to the position
that older children, more so than younger children,
have a tendency to be replaced. However, this happens
only after they have been in care for at least three
years.

The findings concerning ethnicity and replacement
report unexpected results. Table 17 suggests that the
black child is least likely to be replaced. It can be
seen that white children and the "other" category
(Hispanic, Asian, Native American) were far more likely to experience replacement than black children. Only
19 percent of black children experienced unstable care,
whereas 27 percent of white children and 24 percent of
the children in the "other" category had an unstable
foster care experience. The chi square score for
Table 17 of 29.89 is statistically significant at the
.001 level.

The impact of length of time in care on the zero
order relationship between number of placements experienced and ethnicity is explored in Table 18. Table 18

TABLE 16

NUMBER OF PLACEMENTS EXPERIENCED BY AGE OF
FOSTER CHILD, CONTROLLED BY
LENGTH OF TIME IN CARE
(PERCENTAGES)

Years in Care

Number of Placements	0 thru 3 years					3 thru 17 years		
	Children's Age in Years					Children's Age in Years		
	$0-1\frac{1}{2}$	$1\frac{1}{2}-3$	$3-6$	$6-13$	$13-17$	$3-6$	$6-13$	$13-17$
1 or 2	86	84	89	80	82	74	70	59
3 or more	14	16	11	20	18	26	30	41
	(240)	(185)	(348)	(712)	(646)	(177)	(918)	(871)

G=.09 $\quad$ G=.23

X^2=15.90 df=4 P<.001 $\qquad$ X^2=30.26 df=2 P<.001

TABLE 17

NUMBER OF PLACEMENTS EXPERIENCED
BY ETHNICITY OF FOSTER CHILD
(PERCENTAGES)

Number of Placements	Black	White	Other*
1 or 2	81	73	76
3 or more	19	27	24
	(1312)	(2441)	(358)

$X^2=29.89$ df=2 P<.001

*Hispanic, Asian, Native American

reports only data on black and white foster children.
The "other" category, consisting of children who were
Hispanic, Asian, or Native American, was dropped from
Table 18 because the variable length of time in care
was not indicated for the majority of these children.
Regardless of this limitation of the data, it can be
observed in Table 18 that a larger percentage of white
children continue to experience unstable care than
black children when time in care is controlled for.
The chi square score of 8.28 for zero through three
years in care is statistically significant at the .05
level; for three through seventeen years, the chi square
score of 58.82 is statistically significant at the .001
level.

Since Table 17, which depicts the relationship between stability of care and ethnicity, had the three
categories of black, white, and "other" and Table 18,
which describes the relationship between stability of
care and ethnicity, controlling for length of time in
care, had only the two categories black and white, it
is difficult to compare results. Consequently, in

TABLE 18

NUMBER OF PLACEMENTS EXPERIENCED BY ETHNICITY
OF THE FOSTER CHILD, CONTROLLED BY
LENGTH OF TIME IN CARE
(PERCENTAGES)

| | Years in Care | | | |
| | 0 thru 3 years | | 3 thru 17 years | |
Number of Placements	Black	White	Black	White
1 or 2	87	81	77	60
3 or more	13	19	23	40
	(536)	(1470)	(741)	(907)

Yule's Q=.18   Yule's Q=.38

X^2=8.28 df=1 P<.05 X^2=58.82 df=1 P<.001

order to compare these findings, a zero order relationship was calculated between stability of care and ethnicity defined only as black and white. These results
are reported in Table 19.

TABLE 19

NUMBER OF PLACEMENTS EXPERIENCED
BY ETHNICITY OF FOSTER CHILD
DEFINED AS BLACK OR WHITE
(PERCENTAGES)

Number of Placements	Black	White
1 or 2	81	73
3 or more	19	27
	(1312)	(2441)

Yule's Q=.22 x^2=6.91 df=1 P<.05

In Table 19, which describes the association between the number of placements experienced and ethnicity of the foster child defined as black or white,
the chi square score is statistically significant at
the .05 level. The Yule's Q score reported suggests
that a low positive association exists between ethnicity and number of placements experienced. This low
positive association holds for zero through three years
in care and increases to a moderate positive level of
association for three through seventeen years in foster
care as reported in Table 18. This additional analysis
helps to increase confidence that ethnicity defined as
black or white is associated with stability of care.
These findings are unique when compared to past research.

The final question explored in this section concerns whether a relationship exists between the number
of placements experienced and sex of the foster child.
The findings for this relationship are reported in
Table 20. The chi square score reported in Table 20

TABLE 20

NUMBER OF PLACEMENTS EXPERIENCED
BY SEX OF FOSTER CHILD
(PERCENTAGES)

Number of Placements	Male	Female
1 or 2	75	77
3 or more	25	23
	(2277)	(2002)

Yule's Q=-.05 X^2=1.83   df=1   NS

is not statistically significant and the Yule's Q score
suggests a negligible relationship between number of
placements experienced and sex of the foster child.
These findings support those reported by Fanshel and
Shinn.

The above analyses of the questions explored in
this section have proved to be fruitful. A picture of
the child likely to experience stable or unstable care
has begun to develop. Most of the findings tell more
about the child likely to experience unstable care than
the child likely to experience stable care.

Clearly the child who is confronted with behavioral
or emotional problems is a prime candidate for unstable
care. He/She is also probably white and is just as
likely to be male as female. After this child has
spent at least three years in care, the child's age
seems to have an impact on replacement. This finding
suggests that older children are not replaced more
often in care than younger children simply because they
have been in care longer. Rather, the child's age
throughout a major portion of the foster care experience impacts the stability of care. This may be partially attributed to the possibility that the behaviors associated with the various stages of a child's
development are more likely to cause placement breakdown

as the child grows older. For example, the behaviors associated with adolescence are more apt to cause a placement to break down than the behaviors associated with infancy.

It was surprising to find that the exceptional child does not appear to be any more likely to experience unstable care than stable care. An unexpected finding was that the black child is a prime candidate for stable foster care. The child experiencing stable care also is likely to have less than three years in the foster care system. After three years in this system, the chance for unstable care goes up; however, for periods beyond three years, the chance for unstable care remains approximately the same. This is one of the more important findings of the research thus far.

Finally, looking back to the data on the personal characteristics of the research sample, the majority of these youngsters experienced stable foster care. This important finding is similar to research findings reported in other studies on foster care.

The Natural Family

As discussed earlier in this research, it was assumed that various kinds of problems in the natural families of children in foster care may have an impact on the stability of foster care. It was suggested that this linkage might be through: (1) family problems resulting in unclear role expectations for the child, thus creating the likelihood that the child will experience replacement, (2) problems in the natural family that make it difficult for the foster child to have developed adequate coping skills and behaviors for successful placement in care, and (3) particular problems in the family resulting in parental behaviors that cause breakdown of placement because of contact with the child while in care or contact with the child's foster family. The problems causing foster care will be treated as the general problems facing the foster children's natural families. The following questions will be explored concerning these problems:

1. Is unstable foster care positively associated with placement in foster care because a child has been abused, neglected, or abandoned ?

2. Is unstable foster care positively associated with placement in foster care due to alcoholism of the father or mother, drug addiction of the mother, emotional problems of the parents, mental illness of the parents, or conflict between the child and parents ?

Table 21, illustrating the association between number of placements experienced and child abuse defined as a problem causing care, shows a low positive relationship between number of placements experienced and child abuse as a cause of care. It can also be observed that 24 percent of the children having "no" checked for abuse as a cause of care experienced three or more placements, whereas 28 percent who had "yes" checked experienced the same number of placements; only four percentage points separate these two groups.

TABLE 21

NUMBER OF PLACEMENTS EXPERIENCED BY CHILD
ABUSE DEFINED AS A PROBLEM CAUSING CARE
(PERCENTAGES)

Number of Placements	Child Abused	
	NO	YES
1 or 2	76	72
3 or more	24	28
	(3637)	(651)
Yule's Q=.10 X^2=3.70 df=1 NS		

Since the chi square score is not statistically significant, the above findings may be due to chance and give little or no support for a relationship existing between stability of care and child abuse as a cause of foster care.

Number of placements experienced and child neglect as a cause of care were also found to be unrelated. This finding is reflected through Table 22. The Yule's

60

Q score reported in this table is only .03. The percentages reported for children having "no" or "yes" checked for this problem as a cause of care who experienced three or more placements are nearly identical. The chi square score of .44 is not statistically significant.

TABLE 22

NUMBER OF PLACEMENTS EXPERIENCED
BY CHILD NEGLECT DEFINED AS A
PROBLEM CAUSING CARE
(PERCENTAGES)

Number of Placements	Child Neglected	
	NO	YES
1 or 2	76	75
3 or more	24	25
	(2394)	(1895)
Yule's Q=.03	X^2=.44 df=1 NS	

Table 23, depicting the association between number of placements experienced and child abandonment defined as a problem causing care, also suggests that no relationship exists between these two variables. Even though the Yule's Q score of .11 is in the low positive range, the chi square score reported of 3.43 is not statistically significant. Of those children having "no" checked for child abandonment as a cause of care, 23 percent experienced unstable care, with 27 percent experiencing unstable care who had "yes" checked. Consequently, it is concluded from the data that stability of care and abandonment as a cause of care appear to be unrelated factors.

The analyses of the results between stability of foster care and placement in care because of abuse, neglect, or abandonment clearly show that these factors are not related to replacement. As developed earlier in this study, these three factors were thought to

61

TABLE 23

NUMBER OF PLACEMENTS EXPERIENCED BY CHILD ABANDONMENT DEFINED AS A PROBLEM CAUSING CARE
(PERCENTAGES)

Number of Placements	Child Abandoned	
	NO	YES
1 or 2	77	73
3 or more	23	27
	(3730)	(558)

Yule's Q=.11 x^2=3.43 df=1 NS

reflect a breakdown in parental role performance, thus impacting the role performance of the child in foster care. Such a linkage does not appear to exist.

Moving to question 2 in this section, it can be observed in Table 24, which defines the number of placements experienced by father's alcoholism as a cause of care, that a low positive association exists between these two factors. The chi square score reported for Table 24 of 5.38 is statistically significant at the .05 level. Twenty-nine percent of the children having "yes" indicated for this problem as a cause of care experienced three or more placements and 23 percent having "no" checked experienced the same number of placements.

Table 25 reports that number of placements experienced is positively associated with mother's alcoholism defined as a problem causing care. The Yule's Q score

TABLE 24

NUMBER OF PLACEMENTS EXPERIENCED BY FATHER'S
ALCOHOLISM DEFINED AS A
PROBLEM CAUSING CARE
(PERCENTAGES)

Number of Placements	Father's Alcoholism as a Cause of Foster Care	
	NO	YES
1 or 2	77	71
3 or more	23	29
	(3894)	(394)

Yule's Q=.16 X^2=5.38   df=1   P<.05

of .18 suggests that the strength of this association
is in the low positive range. The chi square score of
8.84 is statistically significant at the .01 level.
It can be observed that 23 percent of the children
having "no" checked for this problem experienced three
or more placements, with 30 percent of those having
"yes" indicated experiencing the same number of placements.

Before exploring the data for the remaining problems in question number 2, time in care will be implemented as a control variable in the above relationships,
suggesting that alcoholism of either parent of the
child is related to stability of foster care. By controlling for time in care, these zero order relationships found between stability of care and alcoholism
of either natural parent can be viewed with more confidence.

TABLE 25

NUMBER OF PLACEMENTS EXPERIENCED BY MOTHER'S
ALCOHOLISM DEFINED AS A
PROBLEM CAUSING CARE
(PERCENTAGES)

Number of Placements	Mother's Alcoholism as a Cause of Foster Care	
	NO	YES
1 or 2	77	70
3 or more	23	30
	(3822)	(466)

Yule's Q=.18 x^2=8.84 df=1 P<.01

Table 26 shows the association between number of placements experienced and father's alcoholism as a cause of care, with time in care controlled for. In the first three years of care, it can be observed that the zero order relationship does not hold, the Yule's Q score is reduced to 0, and the chi square score of .02 is not statistically significant. The percentage of children having "no" or "yes" checked who experienced unstable care is identical. For three through seventeen years, the Yule's Q score of .15 remains in the low positive range but the chi square score is not statistically significant; however, this score is nearing statistical significance at the .10 level. It can be observed for the three through seventeen year time period that 32 percent of those children having "no" checked for this problem and 39 percent who had "yes" checked experienced unstable care.

Table 27, which depicts the relationship between number of placements experienced and mother's alcoholism defined as a problem causing care, controlling for time in care, reports that the zero order relationship is replicated. The Yule's Q score suggests a low positive relationship for zero through three years with a chi square score statistically significant at the

TABLE 26

NUMBER OF PLACEMENTS EXPERIENCED BY FATHER'S ALCOHOLISM
DEFINED AS A PROBLEM CAUSING CARE, CONTROLLED
BY LENGTH OF TIME IN CARE
(PERCENTAGES)

	Years in Care			
	0 thru 3 years		3 thru 17 years	
Number of Placements	Father's Alcoholism as a Cause of Foster Care		Father's Alcoholism as a Cause of Foster Care	
	NO	YES	NO	YES
1 or 2	82	82	68	61
3 or more	18	18	32	39
	(2102)	(222)	(1685)	(160)

Yule's Q=0
X^2=.02 df=1 NS

Yule's Q=.15
X^2=2.47 df=1 NS

65

TABLE 27

NUMBER OF PLACEMENTS EXPERIENCED BY MOTHER'S ALCOHOLISM
DEFINED AS A PROBLEM CAUSING CARE, CONTROLLED
BY LENGTH OF TIME IN CARE
(PERCENTAGES)

	Years in Care			
	0 thru 3 years		3 thru 17 years	
	Mother's Alcoholism as a Cause of Foster Care		Mother's Alcoholism as a Cause of Foster Care	
Number of Placements	NO	YES	NO	YES
1 or 2	83	75	70	63
3 or more	17	25	30	37
	(2067)	(257)	(1647)	(198)
	Yule's Q=.23		Yule's Q=.16	
	X^2=10.00 df=1 P<.01		X^2=4.67 df=1 P<.05	

.01 level. For three through seventeen years, the Yule's Q score of .16 shows that the zero order relationship remains at a low positive level. The chi square score of 4.65 is again statistically significant at the .05 level. Thus, the relationship between alcoholism of the mother and stability of care continues to hold when time in care is controlled for.

The above findings clearly show that stability of foster care and mother's alcoholism are related. However, the factor of time in foster care appears to specify when stability of care and father's alcoholism are associated; this is during the three through seventeen year period of time in foster care. It must be noted again that the chi square score for this time period was not statistically significant at the .05 level; however, it was nearing statistical significance at the .10 level. A brief discussion about these interesting findings follows.

A recent study by Slobada appears to give some insight into why alcoholism of parents impacts replacement in foster care. Slobada found that children were negatively affected by alcoholism of their parents in the following ways: (1) the shift of parental roles resulting from alcoholism of either parent causes confusion and complicates the child's role functioning, (2) the inconsistent and unpredictive relationship with the alcoholic parent is depriving, (3) the nonalcoholic parent is disturbed by the alcoholism and therefore is often inadequate in the parental role, and (4) the family's increased social isolation interferes with peer relationships and with emotional support from the extended family.[6]

The first two points clearly suggest that the alcoholic parent is a poor role model for the child. The third point implies that the nonalcoholic parent also has problems in his/her role functioning as parent because of the other spouse's alcoholism. The last point emphasizes the isolation of the family confronted with alcoholism from others, including the extended family. This is, no doubt, a prime reason why the family has trouble functioning effectively.

With the above discussion in mind, a foster child who enters care because of parental alcoholism would appear to have unclear role expectations for functioning in care as well as in other systems. Slobada's

67

study appears to support such a conclusion. That is, Slobada's research seems to suggest that the child's parents provide inadequate roles for the child; the child in turn has problems in role performance resulting in behaviors which are capable of breaking down a foster care placement. Thus the dynamics are established for unstable foster care.

It does not appear to be unusual that the alcoholic mother impacts stability of care regardless of the time the child has spent in care. The mother has been found to be the person having the greatest impact on and involvement with a child's socialization throughout childhood.[7] Consequently, regardless of when a child enters care or how long the child remains in care, the effects of the mother's alcoholism continue to have an impact on the child being replaced.

The findings for father's alcoholism are somewhat more complicated than those for mother's alcoholism. The first issue that comes to mind concerning why father's alcoholism seems to impact replacement only after the child has been in care for at least three years would be related to the factor of the age of the child. Since research reports that the father becomes more active in the child's socialization as the child grows older,[8] the impact of the father's alcoholism would thus be more pronounced on the older child because of this increased involvement. It would seem that those children who have been in care over three years would be much older than those children in care under three years. However, the general distribution of the data reports that the numbers of older children in foster care over three years is relatively similar to the numbers of older children in care less than three years. There is little reason to believe that this distribution would be different for children of alcoholic fathers. Consequently, there appears to be little support for the age of the foster child being the explanation for why father's alcoholism affects replacement of the child after three years in foster care.

A more plausible explanation would seem to be that the father's contact with the child is the cause of placement breakdown. One important source of contact is the visiting patterns of the parents. Unfortunately, the data does not distinguish between visits by either the mother or father. If this information

68

was known, analysis could be done on the father's visiting patterns as related to stability of care. However, even if such data were available, it still is
not clear why this phenomenon occurs only with children in care at least three years. Regardless of this
limitation of the data and until others build on this
exploratory research, it appears that the alcoholic
father's contact with the child may promote unstable
foster care.

Moving to the next problem listed in question 2,
drug addiction of the foster child's mother, it appears
not to be related to the stability of foster care, as
illustrated in Table 28. The Yule's Q score of .03 is

TABLE 28

NUMBER OF PLACEMENTS EXPERIENCED BY DRUG
ADDICTION OF FOSTER CHILD'S MOTHER
DEFINED AS A PROBLEM CAUSING CARE
(PERCENTAGES)

Number of Placements	Drug Addiction of Child's Mother as a Cause of Foster Care	
	NO	YES
1 or 2	76	75
3 or more	24	25
	(4146)	(142)
Yule's Q=.03	X^2=.02 df=1 NS	

in the negligible range and the chi square score of
.02 is not statistically significant. The percentage
of children having this problem checked as a cause of
care and who experienced three or more placements is
nearly identical to the percentage not having it
checked who experienced unstable care.

Table 29, reporting the relationship between number of placements experienced and emotional problems

of the child's parents defined as a cause of care, also reports a non-statistically significant chi square
score and a negligible Yule's Q score. The percentage
of children having "yes" or "no" checked for this
problem as a cause of care who experienced unstable

TABLE 29

NUMBER OF PLACEMENTS EXPERIENCED BY EMOTIONAL
PROBLEMS OF CHILD'S PARENT(S) DEFINED
AS A PROBLEM CAUSING CARE
(PERCENTAGES)

Number of Placements	Parent(s)' Emotional Problems as a Cause of Foster Care	
	NO	YES
1 or 2	76	75
3 or more	24	25
	(2734)	(1554)

Yule's Q=.03 X^2=.40   df=1   NS

care is again nearly identical.

An association between the next problem explored,
mental illness of the child's parents, and stability
of care is also found not to exist. Table 30 shows
a Yule's Q score of .08, which is again in the negligible range, and a chi square score of 2.13, which is
not statistically significant. There is only a three
percentage point difference separating those children
who experienced three or more placements with either
"no" or "yes" indicated for this problem.

Finally, Table 31, depicting the relationship between number of placements experienced and conflict between the child and parent defined as a problem causing
care, suggests that these two factors are unrelated.

70

TABLE 30

NUMBER OF PLACEMENTS EXPERIENCED BY MENTAL
ILLNESS OF CHILD'S PARENT(S) DEFINED
AS A PROBLEM CAUSING CARE
(PERCENTAGES)

Number of Placements	Mental Illness of Parent(s) as a Cause of Foster Care	
	NO	YES
1 or 2	77	74
3 or more	23	26
	(3654)	(634)

Yule's Q=.08 X^2=2.13 df=1 NS

TABLE 31

NUMBER OF PLACEMENTS EXPERIENCED BY CONFLICT
BETWEEN CHILD AND PARENT(S) DEFINED
AS A PROBLEM CAUSING CARE
(PERCENTAGES)

Number of Placements	Child and Parent(s) Conflict as a Cause of Foster Care	
	NO	YES
1 or 2	76	74
3 or more	24	26
	(3568)	(720)

Yule's Q=.05 X^2=1.12 df=1 NS

The Yule's Q score is negligible, and the chi square score is again not statistically significant. Approximately one quarter of the children who had "no" or "yes" checked for this problem as a cause of care experienced unstable foster care.

The above analysis of certain family problems suggests that parental alcoholism appears to be the only factor impacting stability of care. Mother's alcoholism was found to be associated with replacement regardless of the time the child spent in foster care. However, father's alcoholism seemed to have an impact only after the child had been in care at least three years. The explanation for how these factors may be related was also discussed.

The final two questions of importance under the social component, the child's natural family, focus on the relationship between the stability of foster care and the visiting patterns of the natural parents and also the intactness of the child's natural family. The impact of visiting on replacement is explored basically because of the research done by Fanshel and Shinn suggesting that visiting by parents may disrupt continuity of care. The association between stability of foster care and the intactness of the natural family is analyzed due to the possibility, discussed earlier, that the foster child from the non-intact family may have learned role behaviors that are inappropriate for dealing with a two parent family system which is the case for most foster families. The questions explored are as follows:

3. Is unstable foster care positively associated with the number of times parents visit the child in care ?

4. Is unstable foster care positively associated with the natural family which is not intact ?

It can be observed in Table 32, which depicts the association between the stability of care and visiting by the natural parents, that no association exists between these two factors. The gamma score of -.03 is in the negligible range and the chi square score of 5.42 is not statistically significant. In each category under number of times visited by the parents, the difference in percentages for children who experienced unstable care varies only slightly. These findings

72

TABLE 32

NUMBER OF PLACEMENTS EXPERIENCED BY NUMBER OF TIMES
NATURAL PARENTS VISITED FOSTER CHILD
(PERCENTAGES)

Number of Placements	Number of Visits by Natural Parents*				
	No visit	1 to 2	3 to 4	5 to 61	
1 or 2	79	76	74	82	
3 or more	21	24	26	18	
	(1336)	(387)	(203)	(157)	

G=-.03 X^2=5.42   df=3   NS

*Visiting patterns were recorded for a three month period. The term "natural parent" is substituted in the table for the term "principal child-caring person" indicated on the survey questionnaire.

73

give no support to the somewhat alarming possibility, reported by Fanshel and Shinn, that visiting by parents may disrupt foster care. However, one must be alerted again to the limitations of the data; the visiting patterns only cover a three month time period.

Little support is found in the data for a relationship existing between stability of foster care and intactness of the child's natural family.[9] This conclusion is based on the findings in Table 33. The Yule's Q score of .09 suggests that the relationship of these two variables is positive; however, this association is in the negligible range. The chi square score is statistically significant at the .05 level,

TABLE 33

NUMBER OF PLACEMENTS EXPERIENCED BY INTACTNESS
OF FOSTER CHILD'S FAMILY
(PERCENTAGES)

Number of Placements	Family Intact	Family not Intact
1 or 2	81	78
3 or more	19	22
	(425)	(2037)
Yule's Q=.09	X^2=4.58 df=1 P<.05	

thus giving a degree of confidence that the findings in Table 33 are not due to chance. The results for this table concerning intact or non-intact families also imply that a slightly higher percentage of children from non-intact families experienced unstable foster care. Even though these findings give very limited support to the impact of the intactness of the natural family on the stability of care, this impact appears so slight that it is of little or no consequence.

Drawing the analyses of the findings together under the social component, the child's natural family, little evidence was found for a linkage existing

74

between the natural family and the stability of foster care. Only parental alcoholism was found to be associated with stability of care. The above findings downplay the importance of the natural family in determining the stability of foster care. The importance of these findings will be discussed in greater detail in the chapter to follow.

The Agency

In this final section, the social service agency is the point of concern. The main emphasis will be to discover if the social service agency appears to be reacting to the problem of replacement; secondary emphasis is placed on whether the social service agency appears to impact replacement.

The first question will attempt to ascertain if the agency appears to be reacting to the special problems of children experiencing unstable care by assigning caseworkers to these children with advanced education and experience. As discussed earlier, it is assumed that caseworkers with these particular qualifications will be better skilled at dealing with the special needs of children who have experienced unstable foster care. The following question deals with this issue:

1. Are caseworkers with advanced education and experience more apt to be assigned to children experiencing unstable care than caseworkers not having advanced education and experience ?

Table 34, which describes the relationship between educational level of the caseworker and number of placements experienced, reports that no relationship appears to exist between these two factors. The contingency coefficient is negligible and the chi square score is not statistically significant. These results clearly give no indication that a concerted effort is made to match workers having advanced education with children who have experienced unstable foster care.

TABLE 34

EDUCATION LEVEL OF CASEWORKER BY NUMBER
OF PLACEMENTS EXPERIENCED
(PERCENTAGES)

Education Level of Caseworker	Number of Placements	
	1 or 2	3 or more
High School Graduate	2	2
Junior College Graduate	1	1
Bachelor of Social Work	15	14
Bachelor Degree other than Social Work	42	46
Some Graduate Work	21	20
Master of Social Work or Doctorate of Social Work	13	11
Graduate Degree other than Social Work	5	5
Other	1	1
	(2784)	(940)

Contingency Coefficient=.00
x^2=10.85 df=7 NS

76

In Table 35, a similar picture is presented for the relationship between years of experience of the caseworker and number of placements a child experiences while in care. The gamma score reported is in the

TABLE 35

YEARS OF EXPERIENCE OF CASEWORKER BY
NUMBER OF PLACEMENTS EXPERIENCED
(PERCENTAGES)

Number of Years of Experience of Caseworker	Number of Placements	
	1 or 2	3 or more
0 to 1	17	15
1 to 4	34	32
4 to 7	21	23
7 to 10	16	15
10 to 13	6	7
13 to 16	3	4
16 to 40	3	4
	(2718)	(924)

$G=.07$ $X^2=7.25$ $df=6$ NS

negligible range and the chi square score is not statistically significant. As found for the caseworker's educational level, there is no indication of an overt effort to assign workers with advanced experience to children confronted with unstable foster care.

The final question explored deals with the impact of the agency on the problem of replacement as reflected through the number of times caseworkers are assigned to a foster child. The question is as follows:

2. Is unstable foster care positively associated with caseworker turnover ?

Table 36, which depicts the association between number of placements experienced and the number of caseworkers assigned, does indeed show that a moderate positive association exists between these two factors as reflected by the gamma score of .30. The chi square score of 110.13 is statistically significant at the .001 level. Clearly, the percentage of children who have experienced three or more placements increases with the number of caseworkers assigned.

However, Table 37, which shows the relationship between number of placements experienced and number of caseworkers assigned, with time in care controlled for, implies that the factor of length of time in care specifies when the zero order relationship holds. It can be seen that for the first three years in care, the gamma score remains at the .30 level and the chi square score of 59.83 is also statistically significant at the .001 level. After three years in care, the zero order relationship no longer holds; this is reflected by the gamma score of .06 which is at the negligible level and the chi square score which is not statistically significant.

The above results indicate that stability of foster care is associated with caseworker turnover for only the first three years of care; that is, during this time period, the more workers assigned to a child, the greater the possibility of this child being replaced. After three years in care, this association is no longer present. These findings appear to give some support to Shapiro's position that caseworker turnover has a negative impact on the client because it may play a role in the replacement process.

However, the association between caseworker turnover and replacement is far from clear and other explanations for this relationship are possible. One would be that the child who continually breaks down his/her placements is assigned to different workers with the intent that they might be more successful in preventing the cycle of replacement. Regardless of such possibilities, the more important issue is that caseworker turnover and replacement are associated during the first three years of foster care. From the viewpoint of the foster child experiencing unstable care, he/she not only lacks continuity with foster parents, but also has a tendency to lack continuity with caseworkers.

TABLE 36

NUMBER OF PLACEMENTS EXPERIENCED BY NUMBER
OF CASEWORKERS ASSIGNED
(PERCENTAGES)

Number of Placements	Number of Caseworkers Assigned			
	1	2	3 to 4	5 or more
1 or 2	85	81	72	66
3 or more	15	19	28	34
	(832)	(1078)	(1094)	(900)
	G=.30	X^2=110.13	df=3	P<.001

TABLE 37

NUMBER OF PLACEMENTS EXPERIENCED BY NUMBER
OF CASEWORKERS ASSIGNED, CONTROLLED
BY LENGTH OF TIME IN CARE
(PERCENTAGES)

	Years in Care							
	0 thru 3 years				3 thru 17 years			
	Number of Caseworkers Assigned				Number of Caseworkers Assigned			
Number of Placements	1	2	3 to 4	5 or more	1	2	3 to 4	5 or more
1 or 2	88	84	75	71	70	72	71	65
3 or more	12	16	25	29	30	28	29	35
	(687)	(742)	(549)	(171)	(132)	(263)	(512)	(700)

0 thru 3 years:
G=.30
X^2=59.83 df=3 P<.001

3 thru 17 years:
G=.06
X^2=7.44 df=3 NS

The above findings give little indication that the social service agency attempts to react to the special needs of children experiencing unstable care by the assignment of caseworkers with advanced education and experience. It was also discovered that unstable care appears to be related to caseworker turnover during the first three years of the foster care experience.

Summary

The data suggests that the foster care system is a relatively stable system in which most children experience only one or two placements. Even though others have found a similar picture in their research, the foster care system continues to be seen as a system that burdens large numbers of children with discontinuity and disruption resulting from frequent changes in placement.

The relationship between time in care and replacement emerged as an interesting research finding. One would think that the more time a child spends in care, the greater the number of placements the child would experience. Such appears not to be the exact case. The data suggests that after three years in care, the impact of time on stability of care remains about the same through seventeen years. The substantial breaking point between children experiencing stable or unstable foster care appears to be right at three years in care. This finding suggests that there is surprisingly great continuity of care for many children once they move past the three year time period.

The findings under the social component, the child, reported the greatest number of factors appearing to have a relationship with the stability of foster care. Little linkage was found between stability of care and the child's natural family; also, the social service agency does not appear to react to the special needs of children experiencing unstable care by assigning them workers with advanced education and experience. One factor analyzed under the social service agency, caseworker turnover, was found to be associated with unstable foster care.

81

Notes and References

1. Shirley M. Vasaly, Foster Care in Five States: A
    Synthesis and Analysis of Studies from Arizona,
    California, Iowa, Massachusetts, and Vermont
    (Washington, D.C.: George Washington University,
    Social Work Research Group, 1976).

2. David Fanshel and Eugene Shinn, Children in Foster
    Care: A Longitudinal Investigation (New York: Col-
    umbia University Press, 1978), p. 139.

3. Alan P. Gruber, A Study of Children, Their Biolog-
    ical and Foster Parents (Springfield, Massachu-
    setts: Governor's Commission on Adoption and Fos-
    ter Care, 1973), p. 17.

4. These findings do not necessarily refute the Gru-
    ber research on the positive relationship found
    between handicapped children and replacement. In
    Gruber's research, the children were not placed
    because of the child's handicap but instead for
    other reasons. Gruber also defined the child's
    handicap in broader terms, that included, among
    other things, physical disabilities and mental
    retardation. Thus the present findings and Gru-
    ber's results appear not to be comparable because
    of these issues.

5. A variation of these findings was reported by the
    author in the article, "The Association of Demo-
    graphic Variables with the Stability of Foster
    Family Care," Psychology: A Quarterly Journal of
    Human Behavior 17 (Winter 1980):31-5.

6. S. Slobada, "The Children of Alcoholics: A Ne-
    glected Problem," Hospital and Community Psychi-
    atry 25 (1974):605-6.

7. F. Ivan Nye, Role Structure and Analysis of the
    Family (Beverly Hills, CA: Sage Publications,
    1976), p. 36.

8. Ibid., p. 153.

9. A variation of these findings was reported by
    the author in the article, "Marital Status and
    Family Source of Income: Potential Predictors

for Determining the Stability of Foster Family Care ?," <u>Adolescence</u>, in press.

CHAPTER V

THE FINDINGS: AN UNDERSTANDING,
IMPLICATIONS, AND OVERVIEW

In the beginning of this research, it was stated that a variety of studies have reported findings on factors associated with foster children who return to their natural families or who have been adopted, both outcomes of foster care viewed by many as positive. However, little research has been conducted on identifying factors related to the problem of concern in this study--the identification of variables associated with stable or unstable foster care.

As discussed earlier in this research, professionals working in the foster care system generally believe that if a child must remain in foster care because other alternatives are not available, the fewer the number of foster homes the child experiences, the better off the child will be. A limited number of studies appear to give support to this position.

As the data was analyzed, it was discovered that the number of children who experienced unstable foster care, defined as three or more placements, was considerably less than one would expect, roughly one-fourth of the sample. Even though this figure represents many children who are confronted with unstable foster care, in terms of the total system, children who experience unstable care are an exception to the rule.

This relatively stable picture does not deny the importance of the problem of replacement of foster children or the need for additional research on this problem. It must be recalled that the children in this sample who experienced three or more placements represent literally thousands of youngsters in the foster care system throughout the United States. This study has been the first major effort to isolate factors associated with multiple replacement of these children. Much has been learned about those children who experience stable foster care as well.

This chapter will recapitulate the key findings of this research, will attempt to make sense out of these findings through the development of a theoretical perspective, and will also discuss the implications of these findings for those concerned with the foster care system.

Key Findings

The research problem was approached through the use of three social components appearing to have relevance for understanding the problem of stability of foster care--the foster child, the foster child's natural family, and the agency providing the foster care service. An effort was made to discover what type of child appears to experience stable or unstable care and the general characteristics of his/her natural family. The social service agency was mainly viewed from the perspective of how it reacts to the child experiencing stable or unstable foster care.

Naturally not all of the potentially relevant variables for understanding the stability of foster care were analyzed. However, the number of variables explored appears to give new insight into the problem of stability of foster care. It is hoped that others will continue to build on what has been found in this study or will explore those factors not included in this work.

With these limitations in mind, the following conclusions are presented which summarize the findings from the preceding chapters:

1. The majority of the children, over 75 percent of the research sample, experienced stable foster care, one or two placements

2. The factor of time in foster care impacts the sta- bility of care at the three year mark. Children who have been in care for at least three years have a much greater chance of experiencing unstable care than children in foster care less than three years. However, the proportion of children experiencing unstable care for anywhere from three up to seven- teen years remains about the same

3. Age becomes a factor related to number of place- ments experienced after foster children have been in care at least three years

4. The white foster child has the greatest tendency toward unstable foster care, the black foster child

the least tendency

5. A child's gender appears to be unrelated to sta-
    bility of foster care

6. Children who have been defined as being confronted
    with behavioral or emotional problems have a tend-
    ency to experience unstable foster care

7. The child who has been defined as a juvenile delin-
    quent or as a status offender, or who is defined as
    exceptional, does not appear to be more likely to
    experience unstable foster care than the foster
    child not confronted with these problems

8. With the exception of parental alcoholism, prob-
    lems in the natural family do not appear to impact
    stability of foster care

9. Children who experience unstable foster care are
    not any more likely than children who experience
    stable care to have workers assigned to them with
    advanced experience and education

10. Children in foster care three years and under who
    experience caseworker turnover have more of a tend-
    ency to experience unstable foster care than chil-
    dren in foster care over three years.

        With the above findings in mind, an effort will
be made to integrate these findings into a very basic
theoretical perspective.

                Toward an Understanding of
                  Stability of Foster Care

        The literature on the foster care system is near-
ly devoid of theory attempting to explain or interpret
phenomena related to this system. Given this state,
much of the research concerned with foster care issues
has been at the exploratory level; the present study
has been no exception.

        An effort will be made to translate the findings
of this study into some speculative reasoning providing interpretation and explanation about the problem of stability of foster care. Such an analysis
will provide the building blocks for a theoretical

understanding of the problem of concern. It is hoped
that others will build on this theoretical perspective.

The System

Clearly the foster care system has been found in
this study to be a very stable system that appears to
provide continuity of care for most of the children who
enter it. This finding suggests that the foster care
system appears to honor the value that a stable environment is far more conducive to positive child development than an unstable environment. Even though the
children have had their lives disrupted by placement in
care because of problems in their natural families, on
the whole, the belief that a stable environment is important for a child's development appears to be a reality for most foster children once in the system.

The general feeling, however, as discussed earlier, is that most children in foster care are constant-
ly moved. Another general belief appears to be that
this is one of the prime causes of why many foster
children supposedly have high rates of behavioral and
emotional problems.[1] The findings in this study appear
to challenge the notion that foster children are confronted with high numbers of replacements, thus suggesting that the alleged high rate of behavioral or emotional problems found among foster children is due to
other factors.

Adding to this stable picture is the way in which
time in care impacts the phenomenon of replacement. As
would be expected, the factor of length of time in care
influences replacement, however not in the sense one
would think. The assumption, discussed earlier, stat-
ing that the longer the time a child spends in care,
the greater the number of placements experienced, does
not appear to be correct. The results of this study
have reported that at the three year point in care a
pronounced tendency toward replacement occurs; however,
this tendency remains about the same at any point after
three years in care on up to seventeen years. In essence, a higher percentage of children are replaced
after three years in care than before, yet this percentage remains very similar from three years on up to
seventeen years, a finding far from expected.

Even though the goal of reuniting the child with

his/her natural family is often not met, the value attached to the importance of maintaining a stable environment for a child's development appears to be a reality for most children placed in the foster care system. However, it should be kept in mind that the foster care system is a less than ideal environment for any child. Fortunately, at least it can be concluded from this research that most children who enter this system are spared unnecessary movement.

The Child

Of the three social components studied in this research, the foster child emerged as the social component providing the greatest insight into the problem of stability of foster care. This conclusion is based on the fact that of the three social components, a greater number of variables explored under the social component, the child, was found to be related to stability of care. The other two social components, the natural family and the social service agency, produced fewer variables related to stability of care. However, the list of variables explored under these two social components was far from exhaustive, suggesting that the above conclusion should be viewed with caution.

If we look at specific variables found to be positively associated with unstable foster care under the social component, the child, the variables or characteristics coming through as correlates clearly related to unstable care are behavioral and emotional problems. One would assume that children with these types of problems, more so than other foster children, are difficult for foster parents to care for.

Unfortunately, one of the major limitations of the data is that information was not available on foster parents. No doubt, foster parents play an important role in determining if a child experiences replacement or not. It appears reasonable to speculate that one known characteristic of foster parents reported by other research that may help to explain why children with behavioral and emotional problems are prime candidates for replacement is the lack of training these parents receive to do their job.[2] Seemingly, when a child with behavioral or emotional problems is placed with foster parents who do not have training in dealing with the special needs of this child, the

probability of placement breakdown increases. This
possibility, as well as other important possibilities
concerning the impact of the foster parent on replacement, will hopefully be explored by others.

Other important characteristics found to be related to stability of foster care under the social component, the child, were ethnicity and age. Surprisingly, black children were found to experience stable foster care in greater numbers than white children. Age
of the child only became a factor after he/she had been
in care at least three years. At most, we can conclude
that the black child has the greatest chance of set-
tling into a stable foster care situation; this would
appear to be positive for the black child. However,
again it should be noted that foster care is a less
than ideal environment for any child, even if the child
experiences only one foster home. With regard to the
variable of age, as suggested earlier in this study,
later stages of a child's development appear to be a
factor contributing to placement breakdown.

Finally, the above discussion concerning the child
as the most fruitful social component for increasing
understanding of the problem of stability of foster
care must be viewed in the context of the total foster
care system. Most children who enter this system experience stable foster care; however, in viewing those
children who do not experience stable care, the results
of this study suggest that the characteristics of these
children, and not their families or the agency providing the foster care service, give the greatest insight
into understanding the phenomenon of replacement.

A Linkage

The findings give little or no support for a
linkage between the child's natural family or the
agency providing the foster care service and the problem of concern, stability of foster care. The only
problem in the foster child's family which appears to
impact replacement is alcoholism of the parents.

Even though it is far from clear how alcoholism
impacts stability of foster care, the linkage between
mother's alcoholism and replacement appears to be related to the important role she plays in the child's
socialization process. Research has reported that this

90

socialization process appears to be less than adequate for the child of the alcoholic mother.[3] The breakdown in the socialization process does not provide the child with adequate role performance needed to function effectively in foster care, as well as in other systems. Consequently, when this child is placed in foster care the child has a tendency to experience replacement.

The linkage of the relationship between father's alcoholism and replacement is thought to be related to the father's contact with the child in care. Kadushin gives some support for this possibility with his suggestion that natural parents are capable of causing replacement to occur through acting out behaviors when they come in contact with their child in placement.[4] The relationship between alcoholism of the father and stability of care was not as strong as the relationship found for mother's alcoholism and number of placements experienced when time in care was controlled for.

The only variable found to be associated with the agency and replacement was caseworker turnover. The data reports that a positive association exists between number of placements foster children experience and the number of caseworkers assigned to these children. No evidence was found for the agency attempting to meet the special needs of the child experiencing unstable care by assigning a worker to this child with advanced education and experience.

Summary

The above analysis has drawn together a sense of understanding of the empirical results of this study. Some of the discussion involved speculative reasoning to explain the problem of stability of foster care. Other parts of the discussion were more concrete and moved beyond speculation. It is felt that several propositions can be formulated about the problem of stability of foster care. Hopefully others will build on these propositions and continue to explore other facets of this problem.

1. The foster care system, when viewed from a macro level, is a relatively stable system in which most children experience continuity of foster care

2. The greatest degree of insight into the problem of

stability of foster care appears to be derived
from focusing directly on the characteristics describing the child

3. The fact that children spend longer periods of
    time in foster care does not necessarily mean that
    these children will experience more replacements

4. The child's natural family has little impact on the
    phenomenon of replacement

5. The social service agency does not necessarily
    assign caseworkers with advanced experience and
    education to children experiencing unstable foster
    care. Furthermore, children who experience case-
    worker turnover during the first three years of
    foster care have a tendency to experience replace-
    ment.

Implications

Several important implications about the foster
care system have emerged from this study. One implication is that the child who is placed in care does
not necessarily continue to experience greater numbers
of placements as time in care increases. Instead,
time in foster care appears to be a dichotomous variable with three years in care being the critical point
at which the chance for replacement greatly increases.
After the three year point, however, the probability
of replacement remains the same up to seventeen years
in care. In essence, this finding provides new insight into how time in care affects the replacement
process.

The findings concerning the natural family and
its effect on stability of foster care appear to have
important implications for future research. A variety
of variables ranging from the intactness of the natural family to problems confronting the natural family
were analyzed in the present study to discover if such
factors affect replacement. Little linkage was found
between the natural family and replacement. However,
the impact of the family on all aspects of a child's
life suggests that factors probably do exist in the
natural family that are related to the number of placements a child experiences. The findings from this
study point to those factors which are not related to

92

replacement; hopefully others will continue to look for factors that are related to replacement.

The social service agency providing the foster care service also needs further exploration. Only a small number of variables was analyzed related to this important element, resulting in the discovery of several key findings. Due to the obvious role of the social service agency in determining if a child experiences stable or unstable foster care, it would appear that more variables related to the agency need to be explored.

Finally, since the majority of foster children have a stable relationship with their foster parents, it must be recognized that many of these children have developed important psychological ties that may be as strong as those developed with their natural parents. Goldstein et al. feels that such strong ties between the foster child and his/her foster parents cannot be broken without harming either the foster parents or, more importantly, the foster child.[5] In essence, according to Goldstein et al., once the psychological relationships form between the child and his/her foster parents, separation from these substitute parents becomes no less painful and no less damaging to a child than the separation form his/her natural parents.[6]

Given the fact that the foster care system provides continuity of care for most children, there appears to be room for giving fuller recognition to the psychological relationship that has formed between many foster children and their foster parents. Goldstein et al. argues that this psychological relationship should be fully legalized by the courts; others have argued that the natural parents come first, regardless of such relationships.[7] A quote from Fanshel and Shinn reflects this strong support in favor of the natural family.

"The termination of parental rights reflects one of the most extreme forms of state power. People should not be penalized because they are poor, because they are mentally ill, or because they are afflicted with drug addiction or alcoholism. They should not be penalized because it is less expensive for society to terminate their rights and allow others, endowed with better economic

93

means to replace them as the parents of their
children."[8]

It would seem reasonable to assume that a balance
might be worked out between the two extremes of a full
legal recognition of the foster parents' psychological
relationship with the child and the position that the
system must always work toward return of the child to
the natural parents. It must be remembered that many
foster children either have no parents or have lost
total contact with their parents. For these children,
especially if adoption is not possible, a permanent
long term foster care home may be the only chance for
a stable familial situation. A fuller recognition of
this fact appears warranted by the courts. In those
situations where the natural parent is known, the agency should continue to work to reunite the child with
the natural family. Only after it is clearly established that such an outcome is not possible and adoption is out of the question, should a recognition of
the foster parents' psychological tie with the child
be considered as the best permanent relationship for
the child.

The recognition that many children will remain in
foster care for long periods of time and that the majority of these children have stable foster care homes
appears to have important implications for the foster
care system. It may be time to allow those foster
parents who will be the child's true psychological parent to assume full parental responsibility in those
cases where the child cannot return home and other more
desirable outcomes are out of the question. In essence,
this is one way that the forgotten children can achieve
an identity within a family setting that is so important to all children.

Overview

It is hoped that this study has added new insight
into the problem of stability of foster care. Even
though it is felt that new understanding of this problem has emerged, it is important that the strengths
and weaknesses of this study be considered. As in most
research, some of the strengths may also be viewed as
weaknesses.

A major strength of this research was the data analyzed, which was from a larger prior study entitled the National Study of Social Services to Children and Their Families. A large number of variables was available for analysis from the National Study. This large body of data allowed extensive exploration of the problem of stability of foster care. It would have been a near impossibility for a sole researcher to collect the amount of data available from the National Study.

However, this extensive body of data also created a problem. It was very difficult to choose for analysis the variables which appeared to be associated with stability of care. The lack of theory concerning stability of foster care further complicated the process of deciding what factors should be included in the research methodology. This lack of theory to guide the research process was partially overcome by keeping the study at an exploratory level and by focusing on three social components appearing to have a logical tie to the problem of concern.

Another limitation is that most of the variables analyzed were at the nominal or ordinal level. Consequently, advanced multivariate techniques were not used. The basic multivariate technique employed was the use of the cross-tabulation table involving trivariate relationships. Additional research based on higher levels of data using advanced multivariate techniques would undoubtedly provide a more comprehensive understanding of stability of care.

A final strength of this study is that it is one of the few studies to take an indepth look at the problem of identifying factors associated with stability of foster care. Within the literature, only one other comparable study can be found. Hopefully, the findings in the present study will motivate other research activities concerning stability of foster care. At a more pragmatic level, it is hoped that the findings will give new insight into how foster care workers and other foster care staff might help to stabilize and increase continuity of care for those children who must remain in foster care.

Notes and References

1. Henry S. Maas, ed., _Social Service Research: Reviews of Studies_ (Washington, D.C.: National Association of Social Workers, 1978), p. 102.

2. Alfred Kadushin, _Child Welfare Services_ (New York: Macmillan Publishing Company, 1980), p. 332.

3. S. Slobada, "The Children of Alcoholics: A Neglected Problem," _Hospital and Community Psychiatry_ 25 (1974):605-6.

4. Kadushin, p. 368.

5. Joseph Goldstein, et al., _Before the Best Interest of the Child_ (New York: Macmillan Publishers, 1979), p. 40.

6. Ibid., p. 41.

7. Ibid., p. 42.

8. David Fanshel and Eugene Shinn, _Children in Foster Care: A Longitudinal Investigation_ (New York: Columbia University Press, 1978), p. 490.

BIBLIOGRAPHY

Ambinder, Walter J. "The Extent of Successive Placements Among Boys in Foster Homes." Child Welfare
(July 1965):397-8.

Babbie, Earl R. The Practice of Social Research. 2nd
ed. Belmont, California: Wadsworth Publishing
Company, 1979.

Baker, John W., and Holzworth, Annette. "Social Histories of Successful and Unsuccessful Children."
Child Development 32 (1961):135-49.

Bell, R.R. Marriage and Family Interaction. Homewood,
Illinois: The Dorsey Press, 1975.

Charnley, Jean. The Art of Child Placement. London:
Oxford Press, 1955.

Davis, James A. Elementary Survey Analysis. Englewood
Cliffs, New Jersey: Prentice-Hall, 1971.

Fanshel, David. "Status Changes of Children in Foster
Care: Final Results of the Columbia University
Longitudinal Study." Child Welfare (March 1976):
143-71.

Fanshel, David, and Maas, Henry. "Factorial Dimensions
of the Characteristics of Children in Placement
and Their Families." Child Development 33 (1962):
123-44.

Fanshel, David, and Shinn, Eugene. Children in Foster
Care: A Longitudinal Investigation. New York:
Columbia University Press, 1978.

Glickman, Esther. Child Placement Through Clinically
Oriented Casework. New York: Columbia University
Press, 1957.

Goldstein, Joseph; Freud, Anna; and Solnit, Albert J.
Before the Best Interests of the Child. New York:
Macmillan Publishers, 1979.

Gruber, Alan R. Children in Foster Care. New York:
Human Sciences Press, 1978.

Gruber, Alan R. Foster Home Care in Massachusetts. Boston: Governor's Commission on Adoption and Foster Care, 1973.

A Handbook for Social Workers: Permanent Planning for Children in Foster Care. Washington, D.C.: U.S. Department of Health and Human Services, 1980.

Hargrave, Vivian; Shireman, Joan; and Connor, Peter. Where Love and Need Are One. Chicago: Illinois Department of Social Services, 1975.

Horejsi, Charles R. Foster Family Care: A Handbook for Social Workers, Allied Professionals, and Concerned Citizens. Springfield, Illinois: Charles C. Thomas, Publisher, 1979.

Jenkins, Shirley. "Duration of Foster Care - Some Relevant Antecedent Variables." Child Welfare 8 (1976):450-5.

Kadushin, Alfred. Child Welfare Services. New York: Macmillan Publishing Company, 1980.

LeMaster, E.E. Parents in Modern America. Homewood, Illinois: The Dorsey Press, 1977.

Littner, Ner et al. Changing Needs and Practices in Child Welfare. New York: Child Welfare League of America, 1960.

Maas, Henry S. "Children in Long-Term Foster Care." Child Welfare (June 1969):213-33.

Maas, Henry S. ed. Social Service Research: Reviews of Studies. Washington, D.C.: National Association of Social Workers, 1978.

Maas, Henry S., and Engler, Richard E. Children in Need of Parents. New York: Columbia University Press, 1959.

Meier, Elizabeth G. "Adults Who Were Foster Children." Children (January-February 1966):16-21.

National Study on Selected Issues of Social Service to Children and Their Families. Washington, D.C.: Children's Bureau, May 1979.

Nye, Ivan F. Role Structure and Analysis of the Family. Beverly Hills, California: Sage Publications, 1976.

Pardeck, John T. "The Association of Demographic Variables with the Stability of Foster Family Care." Psychology: A Quarterly Journal of Human Behavior 17 (Winter 1980):31-5.

Pardeck, John T. "Marital Status and Family Source of Income: Potential Predictors for Determining the Stability of Foster Care ?" Adolescence, in press.

Pine, Vanderlyn R. Introduction to Social Statistics. Englewood Cliffs, New Jersey: Prentice-Hall, 1977.

Shapiro, Deborah. Agencies and Foster Children. New York: Columbia University Press, 1976.

Sherman, Edward A.; Neuman, Renee; and Shyne, Ann W. Children Adrift in Foster Care: A Study of Alternative Approaches. New York: Child Welfare League of America, 1973.

Shyne, Ann W., and Schroeder, Anita G. National Study of Social Services to Children and Their Families. Washington, D.C.: Children's Bureau, 1978.

Slobada, S. "The Children of Alcoholics: A Neglected Problem." Hospital and Community Psychiatry 25 (1974):605-6.

Vasaly, Shirley M. Foster Care in Five States: A Synthesis and Analysis of Studies from Arizona, California, Iowa, Massachusetts, and Vermont. Washington, D.C.: George Washington University, Social Work Research Group, 1976.

Weinstein, E.A. The Self Image of the Foster Child. New York: Russell Sage Foundation, 1960.

Wiltse, K., and Gambrill, E. "Decision-Making Process in Foster Care." Berkeley: University of California School of Social Welfare, 1973.

INDEX

ABOUT THE AUTHOR

John T. Pardeck is currently assistant professor of social work at Arkansas State University. He was formerly reseacher for the Region VI Child Welfare Training Center, Tulane University School of Social Work. His research interests concern child welfare and issues related to child and family development. He is also joint author of Child Welfare Training and Practice: An Annotated Bibliography by Greenwood Press. He has published articles in Psychology, International Journal of Family Therapy, Journal of Sociology and Social Welfare, International Journal of Social Psychiatry, and Family Therapy. Dr. Pardeck received his Ph.D. in social work from Saint Louis University.